Emerging Architecture

Kommende Architektur

Beyond Architainment

Otto Kapfinger

Editor / Herausgeber

SpringerWienNewYork

Az W Architekturzentrum Wien

With special thanks to all the contributing architects, photographers, and the exhibition and catalog team.
Mit besonderem Dank an alle beteiligten Architekturbüros, FotografInnen und das Ausstellungs- und Katalogteam.
O.K.

Contents
Inhalt

Beyond Architainment

GK What can we expect from Emerging Architecture 3, what are the motives for this selection?
OK The third exploration in this series complements the previous ones to form an 'Austrian trilogy'. The diversity of profound attitudes among the younger generation, from Vienna to Vorarlberg, is given a concise outline, with 30 presented teams and 180 analyzed buildings and projects. 'EA 3' offers a supraregionally oriented show window for autonomous and trendsetting positions that not merely exist on paper or in dataspace alone, but also represent a built reality. By no means do I underestimate the intensity of radiation emitted by unbuilt concepts or visionary imagination. However, ideas translated into materiality were a vital criterion for the present selection. For sure, Walter Benjamin once stated that 'The work is the death mask of conception.' But the idealistic perspective applies, in this sharp form, to the autonomous arts at best. At any rate, architecture is a medium not to be used auratically. The real functioning of the conceptional is neither a matter of marginality, nor a pale reflection, but a substantial touchstone for the profession's evolutionary, everyday competence.
All three explorations obviously concentrated not on seeking out elective affinities, but rather on clearly arranging a spectrum of concrete positions, quite unhomogenically. Does this reflect a curator's skepticism

GK Was erwartet uns in Emerging Architecture 3, was sind die Motive der Auswahl?
OK Die dritte Sichtung in dieser Reihe ergänzt die vorangegangenen zu einer ‚österreichischen Trilogie'. Die Vielfalt profunder Haltungen in der jüngeren Generation von Wien bis Vorarlberg ist damit durch 30 vorgestellte Teams und 180 analysierte Bauten und Projekte prägnant umrissen. ‚EA3' bietet ein überregional orientiertes Schaufenster für eigenständige und zukunftsweisende Positionen, die nicht allein am Papier oder im Datenraum aufscheinen, sondern auch gebaute Realität darstellen. Ich unterschätze keineswegs die Strahlkraft ungebauter Konzepte oder visionärer Imagination. Für diese Auswahl war aber die Umsetzung von Ideen ins Materielle ein mitentscheidendes Kriterium. Gewiss, von Walter Benjamin stammt der Satz: ‚Das Werk ist die Totenmaske der Konzeption.' Aber die idealistische Sichtweise gilt in dieser Zuspitzung höchstens für die autonomen Künste. Die Baukunst jedenfalls ist ein angewandtes und antiauratisch zu gebrauchendes Medium. Das reale Funktionieren des Konzeptionellen ist keine Marginalität, auch kein bloßer Abglanz, sondern ein wesentlicher Prüfstein für die evolutionäre, alltägliche Kompetenz der Profession.
In allen drei Sichtungen ging es ja offensichtlich nicht um das Aufspüren von Wahlverwandtschaften, sondern um das Auffächern

about stylistic inventions and trends of whatever kind? Are there any moments that connect the represented teams?

I find it important to counteract a position that simply stares at Vienna. Young teams, in particular, have shown essential accomplishments in what some casually call the 'backwoods'. Measured contextually – in terms of the distance between local norms and standards newly set with buildings – I would see a lot of examples in the Provinces to be more radical and extensive than some of the statements more strongly acknowledged by the publicity of a metropolitan conglomerate. In general, Austria consists of a dense spectrum of mentalities. In addition, three cities in this small country – Vienna, Graz, Innsbruck – have schools of architecture that are clearly different, and another has recently been added in Linz. Finally, the quite different architecture scene in Vorarlberg has also acted as an autonomous informal 'school'.

Is this heterogeneous field not increasingly interspersed with an intellectual cosmopolitanism that enriches production 'back home'?

The international development has been discussed in a lively form everywhere, but such discussions are not quite fundamental analytically. Over the past fifteen years, we have less visionary material on hand in terms of theory or conception that's worthy of emphasis as compared to other countries. There is a considerable asset, however, in the

eines Spektrums konkreter Haltungen, relativ inhomogen. Spiegelt das die Skepsis des Kurators gegenüber jeglichen Stilbildungen und Trends? Gibt es überhaupt verbindende Momente unter den vertretenen Teams?

Wichtig ist mir, der Fixierung auf Wien allein entgegenzuwirken. In der salopp so genannten ‚Provinz‘ gibt es gerade von jungen Teams essentielle Leistungen. Kontextuell gemessen, also an der Distanz zwischen lokaler Norm und einem durch Bauten dort neu gesetzten Maßstab, erscheinen mir etliche Beispiele in den Bundesländern radikaler und weitreichender als so manche der publizistisch viel stärker beachteten Statements im Gemenge der Großstadt. In dem kleinen Österreich gibt es generell ein dichtes Spektrum von Mentalitäten. Wir haben zudem drei Städte mit Architekturuniversitäten, die sich klar voneinander unterscheiden – Wien, Graz, Innsbruck –, zuletzt kam mit Linz eine vierte dazu. Als eigene, informelle ‚Schule‘ wirkte die nochmals ganz anders gestimmte Szene der Baukünstler Vorarlbergs.

Dieses heterogene Feld ist aber doch mehr und mehr von einem intellektuellen Kosmopolitanismus durchsetzt, der die Produktion ‚daheim‘ befruchtet?

Die Auseinandersetzung mit der internationalen Entwicklung verläuft überall lebhaft, ist analytisch aber nicht wirklich tiefgreifend. Wir haben hier in den letzten 15 Jahren weniger theoretisch oder konzeptionell

consistency and determination with which the various temperaments here develop their own models and follow them up over various periods of time for dispersed tasks and standards, allowing them to mature and realizing them at a high technical and creative level. In other words, pretensions harmonized with reality. These are precisely the qualities I would like to make visible with such initial, compact presentations of oeuvres. It is certainly not my intention to construct new categories of style or formal drawers, as at all times has been the forte of art historians dealing with architecture. In the first place, the differences and the classifications are of no interest to me. Rather, my text and the selection of projects attempt to work out individual and typical outlines, as far as possible within a close compass.

I'm interested in some more details. Overall, 'Beyond Architainment' is a generalizing title – in terms of spatial concepts that would exceed trendy amusement. By what means do the presented teams evade being taken in by an omnipresent 'architecture as culture industry'? What does this imply in the long run? Isn't such negation or delimitation a common tendency?

'Emerging Architecture' is not out for spectacular or speculative novelties. Those are best propagated by themselves, or are quickly detected by the media search radars. Such a hysterical propagating and passing of

Visionäres, das gegenüber anderen Ländern originär hervorzuheben wäre. Ein großes Plus liegt dagegen in der Konsistenz und Konsequenz, in der hier verschiedenste Temperamente eigene Leitbilder entwickeln, sie über Zeiträume hinweg für disperse Aufgaben und Maßstäbe verfolgen, reifen lassen, auf hohem technischen und gestalterischen Niveau realisieren. Also die Übereinstimmung von Anspruch und Wirklichkeit. Es sind exakt diese Qualitäten, die ich mit solchen ersten, kompakten Œuvre-Präsentationen sichtbar machen möchte. Es ist dezidiert nicht meine Absicht, neue Stilkategorien oder formale Schubladkästen aufzubauen, wie es seit je die Stärke von Kunsthistorikern, die sich mit Architektur befassen, war. Mich interessieren zunächst nicht die Unterschiede und die Einordnungen. Ich versuche vielmehr, das Individuelle und Typische in Text und Projektauswahl herauszuarbeiten, soweit es in dem kompakten Rahmen eben geht.

Meine Frage ist damit nicht ganz beantwortet. Du gibst ja doch dem Ganzen mit dem Titel ‚Beyond Architainment‘ eine generalisierende Überschrift – im Sinne von Raumkonzepten abseits der trendigen Belustigung. Wodurch entziehen sich diese vorgestellten Teams nun der omnipräsenten Vereinnahmung durch die ‚Kulturindustrie Architektur‘? Was soll damit letztlich gemeint sein? Ist das nicht – als Negation oder Abgrenzung – doch auch eine gemeinsame Tendenz?

slogans and styles to exhaust an 'economy of attention' (Georg Franck) increasingly marks the publicized reality of architecture. Criticism is strong in Vienna, for instance, of stale and habitual architectural discussions and presentations, and more shows and popular accesses are now being called for. I would again quote Franck, 'In architecture, the circumstance that it has become more important where a house is published than where it is built signalizes the true breakthrough of media esthetics. The common denominator of pluralistically diverse, post-modern architectural styles is that flashiness is cultivated. We have come to see a downright entertainment architecture.'

That statement is entertaining, but isn't it somewhat global? And is it not a liberating sign of strength that many young teams consciously 'surf all the waves' that come in, unlike an old stubborn dogmatism, the unwarranted premises of classic modernity?

Postmodernity happens to be paradox, and actually is a riskier and more sophisticated concept than old modernity. In the end, it means swimming with the tide, venturing on and using its forces – subversively, intelligently, sensually – to make some upstream diversions. That is what applied to Josef Frank's liking for sentimentality and coincidences, that was Alchimia and subsequently Memphis in Italy in the seventies. And then Rem Koolhaas, of course. He was succeeded by the tide of young

‚Emerging Architecture‘ sucht nicht nach spektakulären oder speku-lativen Novitäten. Die werden ohnehin vom medialen Suchradar rasch erfasst oder propagieren sich selbst am besten. Ich suche nicht nach Novität, sondern nach Qualität. Das hysterische Propagieren und Ver-abschieden von Slogans und Stilen im Sinn des Ausreizens der ‚Ökonomie der Aufmerksamkeit‘ (Georg Franck) prägt immer mehr auch die publizistische Realität von Baukunst. In Wien etwa kritisiert man die Fadesse üblicher Architekturdiskussionen und -präsentationen und fordert mehr Show und populäre Zugänge. Da ist natürlich was dran. Aber ich zitiere dazu nochmals Franck: ‚Den eigentlichen Durch-bruch der Medienästhetik signalisiert in der Architektur der Umstand, dass es wichtiger geworden ist, wo die Publikation des Hauses erscheint, als wo es steht. Die pluralistische Vielfalt nachmoderner Architektur-stile hat den gemeinsamen Nenner, dass die Auffälligkeit kultiviert wird. Wir haben inzwischen eine regelrechte Unterhaltungsarchitektur.‘

Ist das nicht auch nur ein unterhaltsames Pauschalurteil? Und – ist es nicht gerade die befreiende Stärke vieler junger Teams, dass sie bewusst ‚alle Wellen reiten‘, die gerade kommen, im Gegensatz zur verbohrten Dogmatik der Alten, der klassischen Moderne?

Postmodernität ist eben paradox, genau genommen ein noch riskanteres, noch anspruchsvolleres Konzept als die alte Modernität. Es heißt

Dutch and their 'fresh conservatism', their equidistant position as regards pragmatism and utopism. Ideological positions were let loose, and approaches to social phenomena and phantasms opened – not in an avant-garde, know-it-all manner, but with a market-conscious smartness that remixes subcultural practices with semiscientific scenarios and handy designs to bring about utterly new hybrids and planning perspectives: an unconventional reading of banalities, processed with 'good marketing'. Dutch topography and its modern 'sprawl' are evidently artificial and even. There is barely anything to compare in Austria, perhaps because we are so strongly confronted with the drama of a 'natural' topos and the largely amodern habitus taken by our own 'sprawl' ...
The young groups, especially in Vienna, do strongly work along that line. The scene is booming, declaring itself in exhibitions, and is initiating a process of 'repoliticization' with autonomous interest groups. Does this indicate that the glittering strategies are being relieved?
There is a lot of competition. Swift and strong positionings are what is required. Again, my insight into this wonderful new surge of ambition is committed to brittleness, not really to catchiness. I marked this out from the beginning. What I'm looking for are positions according to which sustained comfort – provided undramatically – is more important than visual strongman acts; I am fascinated by teams who creatively

letztlich, mit dem Strom zu schwimmen, sich auf ihn einzulassen und seine Kraft subversiv, intelligent, lustvoll zu nützen, um den Strom partiell vielleicht doch dorthin zu führen, wohin er eigentlich nicht wollte. Das war Josef Franks Faible für Sentimentalität und Zufälliges, das war in Italien in den Siebzigern zuerst Alchimia und dann Memphis. Und dann natürlich Rem Koolhaas. In seiner Nachfolge kam die Welle der jungen Niederländer und ihr ‚fresh conservatism‘, ihre Äquidistanz zum Pragmatismus einerseits und zum Utopismus andererseits. Es war das Loslassen ideologischer Positionen, ein offenes Zugehen auf gesellschaftliche Phänomene und Phantasmen – nicht mit avantgardistischem Besserwissen, sondern in marktbewusster Gewitztheit, welche subkulturelle Praktiken mit halbwissenschaftlichen Szenarien und griffigem Design zu ganz neuen Hybriden und planerischen Durchblicken aufmischte: die unkonventionelle Lektüre des Banalen, aufbereitet durch ‚good marketing‘. In Österreich haben wir kaum Vergleichbares, vielleicht weil wir im Gegensatz zur evidenten Künstlichkeit und Flachheit der niederländischen Topografie und ihres modernen ‚sprawls‘ hier stark mit der Dramatik des ‚natürlichen‘ Topos und dem weitgehend amodernen Habitus unseres ‚sprawls‘ konfrontiert sind ...
Die jungen Gruppen, besonders in Wien, arbeiten doch auch sehr in dieser Richtung. Die Szene boomt und deklariert sich in Ausstellungen,

and precisely work on overcoming the architectonic object for the benefit of the architectonic condition; I have come to appreciate architecture that refrains from intentions to convey strong images and effects, but instead wants to form strong sensual aggregates, devoted to qualities that leave behind what can superficially be plotted. The Smithsons said it decades ago: Attention is shifting – from buildings as objects to the contributions they make to spatially condition the emptiness, the territory. In this segment, Austria enjoys a host of first-class examples among the generation between 30 and 45, teams who handle functional things and occupants' requests without being affirmative and who critically go against the grain with programs to be dosed in a clear fashion. They consistently carry out small orders and develop large urbanistic projects alike, not in luxury sections, but by addressing broad, everyday problematical issues, on the pulse of time – no smoke-bombing, no ponderousness of superstructure rhetoric.

In spite of a lack of homogeneity, wefts do seem to be running between the three presentations. Will this densify to an integrated whole at some time, or will the account basically be left unbalanced?

The balance will be left open. 'Vienna Orchestra' is what the Italians called the local scene as early as the 1970s – and it was no thoroughly

beginnt eine ‚Re-Politisierung‘ mit autonomen Interessenverbänden. Sind das Indizien für eine Wachablöse der Glitzerstrategien?

Die Konkurrenz ist groß. Schnelle, starke Positionierung ist gefragt. Mein Blick in diesen wunderbaren neuen Schwall von Ambition gilt wie gesagt dem Spröden, nicht so sehr dem Plakativen. Ich habe das von Beginn an abgegrenzt. Ich suche nach Haltungen, denen nachhaltiger Komfort – undramatisch angeboten – wichtiger ist als der visuelle Kraftakt; mich faszinieren Teams, die kreativ und präzise daran arbeiten, den architektonischen Gegenstand zu überwinden zugunsten des architektonischen Zustandes; ich schätze jene Architektur, die weniger auf starke Bilder und auf Eindruck macht, sondern starke, sinnliche Aggregate formen will im Dienst von Qualitäten, die das vordergründig Abbildbare hinter sich lassen. Die Smithsons sagten es vor Jahrzehnten: Die Aufmerksamkeit verlagert sich – von Gebäuden als Objekten auf den Beitrag, den sie zur räumlichen Konditionierung der Leere, des Territoriums leisten. In diesem Segment gibt es in Österreich in der Generation zwischen 30 und 45 eine Fülle von erstklassigen Beispielen, Teams, die funktionale Dinge und Nutzerwünsche abhandeln, ohne affirmativ zu sein, die Programme kritisch und klar dosiert gegen den Strich bürsten, die vom kleinen Auftrag bis zu großen urbanistischen Projekten Antworten konsistent entwickeln, nicht in Luxussparten,

composed piece back then, but a session of individualists. Today, 'Austrian Diversity' is perhaps more to the point: a diversity of succinct contributions, a higher and dynamic quality of scope, no dichotomy between glittering superstars and a gray mass as in previous times. My role isn't that of a theoretician in retrospection. The people know exactly what they're doing and what they're not. Mine is one out of several contributions. 'Emerging Architecture' guides spotlights to a complex scene. Of course, specialist magazines are quicker in detecting new things and new names. My claim is to selectively deepen the ways the scene is appreciated, to genuinely address the crux, and to enlarge the receptive platform with a touring exhibition and talks about the team abroad. The future of this series remains open…

sondern in alltäglichen, breiten Problemstellungen, am Puls der Zeit, doch ohne Nebelwerfen mit Überbaurhetorik.
Zwischen den drei Präsentationen scheinen in aller Inhomogenität doch thematische Querfäden zu laufen. Wird sich das irgendwann zu einem geschlossenen Ganzen verdichten oder bleibt die Rechnung grundsätzlich offen?
Es bleibt offen. Schon Anfang der 1970er nannten die Italiener die hiesige Szene ‚Vienna Orchestra' – und das war schon damals kein durchkomponiertes Stück, sondern eine Session von Individualisten. Heute ist es eher ‚Austrian Diversity': Vielfalt prägnanter Beiträge, höheres und dynamisches Niveau in der Breite, keine Dichotomie von schillernden Superstars und grauer Masse wie vorher. Meine Rolle ist nicht die des Theoretikers im Nachhinein. Die Leute wissen ganz genau, was sie machen, was nicht. Mein Beitrag ist einer unter anderen. ‚Emerging Architecture' richtet Schlaglichter auf eine komplexe Szene. Natürlich sind die Fachmagazine schneller im Erfassen neuer Dinge, neuer Namen. Mein Anspruch ist, diese Rezeption selektiv zu vertiefen, wirklich jeweils auf den Punkt zu bringen und mit dem Wandern der Ausstellung und mit Vorträgen der Teams im Ausland die rezeptive Plattform zu vergrößern. Die Zukunft der Reihe ist offen…

AllesWirdGut

The five shooting stars up from the country sharing an office in Vienna, in a former grocery store, are anything but affirmatively naïve, as the group's name may suggest. Crystal-clear analyses in urban economy and astonishingly mature planning concepts are behind their zippy project titles, glamorous photomontages and comics perspectives. This is anything but the decorative utopism displayed by a good many architectural pop groups. 'Alles Wird Gut' – all will get well – is rather the motto informing a fresh, impartial approach to seemingly unattractive or cliché-saturated problematic zones. Positive thinking alone is provably not enough in this business. Yet an emotionless awake, vigorous insolence may accelerate considerations of the unwieldy nature of urban realities. Such action may reach the extent of a sober conceptual dynamics that is well considered as a trademark for the AWG projects. Following up on a master's thesis at Vienna's Technical University, for instance, an alternative was elaborated to present infrastructural politics in Bolzano City. Due to the location along the Brenner highway, a major route of EU transit traffic, supraregional transport operators there perceive a need for streamlining. Unlike the plan to dislocate the new high-performance railroad route in terms of an urban 'bypass', AWG calls for a concentration and active cross-linkage of infrastructure in town: 'Bolzano must not be circumvented. The city should benefit from

Urbanity is Synchronism
Urban ist simultan

Die fünf Senkrechtstarter aus der Provinz mit Wiener Büro in einem ehemaligen Lebensmittelladen sind alles andere als affirmativ blauäugig, wie ihr Gruppenname suggerieren könnte. Hinter ihren zackigen Projekttiteln, den glamourösen Fotomontagen und Comic-Perspektiven stecken glasklare stadtökonomische Analysen und erstaunlich reife Planungskonzepte. Nichts liegt hier ferner als der dekorative Utopismus so mancher Architektur-Popgruppen. ‚Alles Wird Gut‘ ist vielmehr ein Motto des frischen, unvoreingenommenen Zugangs auf scheinbar unattraktive oder klischeegesättigte Problemzonen. Positiv denken allein genügt in diesem Geschäft nachweislich nicht. Aber eine emotionslos wache, energiegeladene Unverfrorenheit kann die Auseinandersetzung mit der sperrigen Natur urbaner Wirklichkeiten zu jener sachlichen Konzeptdynamik beschleunigen, die durchaus als Markenzeichen für AWG-Projekte gelten kann. In Weiterführung einer Diplomarbeit an der TU Wien etwa erstellten sie für die Stadt Bozen eine Alternative zur aktuellen Infrastrukturpolitik. Durch die Lage an der Brenner-Route, einer Hauptachse im EU-Transit, ergibt sich dort ein Modernisierungsbedarf der überregionalen Verkehrsträger. Im Gegensatz zur geplanten Auslagerung der neuen Hochleistungsstrasse der Bahn als ‚Bypass‘ der Stadt fordert AWG die Bündelung und aktive Vernetzung der Infrastruktur im inneren Stadtgebiet: ‚Bozen darf nicht umfahren werden. Die Stadt soll von der

DON GIL, Shop Conversion, Graz, 2001
Geschäftsumbau

the high-quality access and thereby make downtown fallows usable. The presence of the traffic system must be accepted and modified such that the problem becomes a potential.' The comics perspectives AWG adopt in this regard play with the euphoric exuberance that propaganda also requires today for visionary urban politics. At any rate, the profoundly argued catalog of measures, the cross and longitudinal sections along the southern railroad bridge over the Eisack, in the central area of the Rome Bridge, and on the completely restructured railroad station site altogether show solid as much as fascinating solutions for traffic ways superimposed with metropolitan occupancies and spatial structures. A project for the Gaudenzdorfergürtel in Vienna strikes the same note – a key juncture of topography and traffic nearby downtown, and a notorious fallow that official planning intends to built back into a public park. In contrast with the custom of dislocating youth culture to the periphery, this is the spot where AWG argues for an adequate densification, to overcome traffic obstacles with an event center. It is this concrete offensive perspective on planning issues, and not a fashionable design appeal, with which groups like AWG are engaged in the renewal of architectural and planning thought.

hochrangigen Erschließung profitieren und damit innerstädtische Brachen nutzbar machen. Die Präsenz der Verkehrsnetze muss akzeptiert und so modifiziert werden, dass das Problem zum Potenzial wird.' Die dazu gezeigten Comic-Perspektiven spielen mit dem euphorischen Überschwang, den Propaganda auch für visionäre Stadtpolitik heute benötigt. Der profund argumentierte Maßnahmenkatalog, die Quer- und Längsschnitte an der Südbrücke der Bahn über den Eisack, im zentralen Bereich der Rom-Brücke und auf dem völlig neu strukturierten Bahnhofsareal zeigen jedenfalls ebenso handfeste wie faszinierende Lösungen – Überlagerungen von Verkehrstrassen mit metropolitanen Nutzungen und Raumstrukturen. In dieselbe Kerbe schlägt ein Projekt für den Gaudenzdorfergürtel in Wien, einem hochrangigen topografischen und verkehrlichen Knoten nahe dem Zentrum – eine notorische Brache, für die offizielle Planungen den Rückbau zu Grünanlagen vorsehen, während AWG im Kontrast zur üblichen Auslagerung von Jugendkultur an die Peripherie gerade hier die adäquate Verdichtung und Überwindung der Verkehrsbarrieren mit einem Veranstaltungszentrum vorschlagen. Es ist diese konkrete, offensive Sicht planerischer Fragen und nicht ein modischer Design-Appeal, mit dem Gruppen wie AWG die Erneuerung des Architektur- und Planungsdenkens betreiben.

DOZ, DORFzentrum, Multipurpose Building, Fließ, interior
Mehrzweckgebäude, Innenraum

Flexible Space, Open Zones
Flexible Freiraumzonen

Conversions of old city centers into traffic-free shopping and tourists' malls have frequently been performed according to trite recipes. The shops' increase in turnover mostly stands opposite to the commercial alienation of old structures – a process of 'gentrification' in which old substance is scenically pepped up, while local societies are hollowed out and superseded. Contrary to the interpretation of the task, the commission itself developing from a small local competition was not at all typical of AWG, declared freaks for cars as they are. Innichen experiences tourist peaks. In the off-season, the center is deserted, and the locals suffer from a hangover following the seasonal stress. The center's novel open space development reacts to these seasonal fluctuations. The varied zones are interactive and can easily be modified. Wooden grates, occupied in summer by streetside cafés, are removed after the season proper and replaced by flowerbed trays. Alternately, individual panels can also be flooded with water, and the vacant spaces that are 'too large' in the off-season are given useful arrangements complemented by a wellness factor. Moreover, resourceful technologies allow the various new surfaces to be undertaken very inexpensively, thus releasing budgets for the 'alternating phases'.

Die Umgestaltung von alten Stadtkernen in verkehrsfreie Shopping- und Touristik-Malls wurde vielfach nach klischeehaften Rezepten vollzogen. Den Umsatzsteigerungen der Läden steht zumeist die kommerzielle Verfremdung der Altstrukturen gegenüber – eine ‚Gentrification‘, die Altsubstanz kulissenhaft aufmöbelt sowie lokale Sozietäten aushöhlt und verdrängt. Für AWG als deklarierte Autofreaks war der aus einem kleinen, lokalen Wettbewerb entstandene Auftrag untypisch, nicht aber dessen Interpretation. Innichen hat touristische Spitzenbelastungen. Außerhalb dieser Saisonen ist das Zentrum wie ausgestorben, die Einheimischen leiden am Hang-over nach dem Saisonstress. Die neue Freiraumgestaltung des Zentrums reagiert auf diese saisonalen Schwankungen. Die verschiedenen Zonen sind interaktiv, können einfach umgestaltet werden. Die Holzroste, im Sommer von Straßencafés besetzt, werden nach der Saison entfernt und durch Erdwannen für Blumenbeete ersetzt. Ebenso können einzelne Platzfelder alternativ mit Wasser geflutet werden, wodurch die in den Zwischensaisonen ‚zu großen‘ Freiräume sinnvolle Gliederungen mit Wellnessfaktor erhalten. Überdies sind die verschiedenen neuen Oberflächen durch findige Technologien extrem kostengünstig ausgeführt und machen damit Budgets für die ‚Wechselphasen‘ frei.

Michaelsplatz; zoning of the center and edges
Zonierung von Mitte und Rand

Michaelsplatz; stone field, light design, platform along the church
Steinfeld, Lichtdesign, Plattform an der Kirche

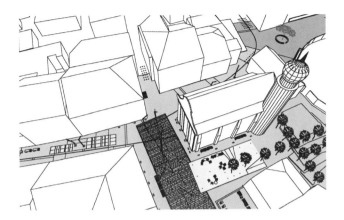

Michaelsplatz; bird's-eye view; details
Vogelschau; Details

urbanity

is

An Open Spatial Node
Offener Raumknoten

A strong implant amidst the traditional village located high above the valley bottom. The small compact construction on a former warehouse site gives a present-day answer to the neighborhood's sturdy old buildings. Like a cliff coming into view through wind and water, the gray-plastered house rises through the vectors of leveling and distance measurements, boundaries of properties and functions, resembling crystal cut angularly on all sides. The interior is amazing in its open rooms, diverse views and vistas. On the crooked slope, the free-standing structure is linked to the exterior level at four different places: a tourists' inquiry office, café, multipurpose hall and exhibition room enjoying separate entrances. The staggered levels can be combined variably inside, but also be interconnected to one single open-plan room. All ways and plateaus then culminate in an open spatial node. The winning contribution to an invited architectural competition – incidentally, one member of the group comes from Fließ – enabled AWG to found their office and materialize their first project. The new building opens the plot instead of occupying it. The house has no thresholds and is accessible on all sides, the street space is arranged without differences in height and continues, as it were, into the inside. Limited costs hindered a planned skin of stone slates. The interior is materially minimal as well: raw and smoothed concrete, wooden panels and wall units.

Ein starkes Implantat inmitten des traditionellen, hoch über dem Talboden gelegenen Dorfes. Der kleine, kompakte Bau an der Stelle eines alten Lagerhauses gibt eine heutige Antwort auf die kräftigen Altbauten der Nachbarschaft. Wie ein Fels durch Wind und Wasser, erscheint das grau geputzte Haus durch die Vektoren von Höhen- und Abstandsbestimmungen, Grundgrenzen und Funktionen nach allen Seiten kantig-kristallin geschliffen. Das Innere verblüfft durch offene Räume, vielfältige Durch- und Ausblicke. Auf dem windschiefen Hang ist der freistehende Bau an vier verschiedenen Stellen mit den Außenniveaus verbunden: Tourismusinfo, Café, Mehrzwecksaal und Ausstellungsraum haben separate Eingänge. Intern können die gestaffelten Ebenen variabel kombiniert, aber auch zu einem einzigen Großraum zusammengeschaltet werden. Dann kulminieren alle Wege und Plateaus im offenen Raumknoten. Das Siegerprojekt im geladenen Architekturwettbewerb – ein Mitglied des Teams stammt aus Fließ – ermöglichte AWG die Bürogründung und die erste Realisierung. Der Platz wird durch den Neubau nicht besetzt, sondern geöffnet. Das Haus ist von allen Seiten schwellenlos betretbar, der Straßenraum ist ohne Höhensprünge gestaltet, setzt sich gleichsam ins Innere fort. Kostenlimits verhinderten die geplante Haut aus Steinplatten. Auch das Innere ist materiell minimal: roher Beton, geschliffener Estrich, Holzpaneele und Schrankwände.

Open interior, five separate levels
Offener Innenraum, fünf separate Ebenen

Ground plans; entrance to the multipurpose hall
Grundrisse; Eingang Mehrzwecksaal

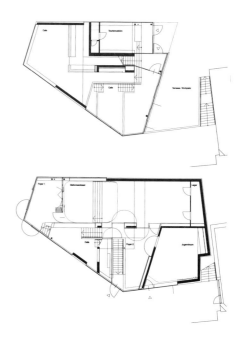

Church parvis; section
Vorplatz zur Kirche; Schnitt

Permanent and maximum exhibition space
Permanente und maximale Ausstellungsfläche

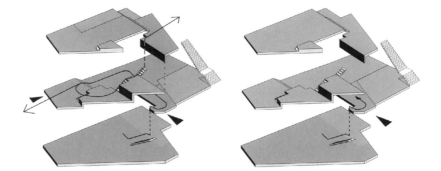

Lower level, permanent exhibition; café and lobby
Untere Ebene, permanente Ausstellung; Café und Foyer

A Problem Becoming a Potential
Problem wird Potenzial

A project commissioned subsequent to the Fließ center and located some 500 m to the west. The south slope is 45° steep, the plot small and the budget minimal. With the help of some friends, the client – a craftsman himself – was able to brick up the walls between the concrete floors. The design takes all of this into consideration, intervenes into the area to the least possible extent, saves on excavated material and expensive concrete work on the slope. While sealing a minimum of soil, it allows the slope to become effective with and within the house. Sixteen steps lead up from the tiny cellar and the entrance area into the main floor, proceeding into a narrow terrace that gives to the south and east. This is half roofed by the upper floor that breaks away from the slope to the north bidding to step out upon a small projecting slope terrace, leading on to the large roof terrace via a pitched roof that covers the staircase. A simple box, perfectly modulated to the topography: a maximum of horizontal surfaces is created upon the most limited space with roofed, shielded and exposed free spaces. The precipice remains perceptible at all levels, is incorporated and made use of in spatial and visual terms. The problem thus turns to become a potential.

Ein Folgeauftrag des Ortszentrums Fließ, ca. 500 m westlich davon gelegen. Der Südhang ist 45° steil, das Grundstück klein, das Budget minimal, der Bauherr – selbst Handwerker – kann mit Freunden zwischen Betondecken die Wände selbst mauern. Der Entwurf bedenkt all dies, greift so wenig wie möglich ins Gelände ein, spart an Aushub und teuren Betonarbeiten im Hang, versiegelt ein Minimum an Erdreich, lässt den Hang mit und im Haus wirksam werden. Vom kleinen Keller und Eingangsbereich geht es 16 Stufen hinauf ins Hauptgeschoß, das nach Süden und Osten in eine schmale Terrasse übergeht. Diese wird zur Hälfte vom Obergeschoß überdacht, das sich nordseitig vom Hang freispielt, dort den Austritt auf eine kleine, auskragende Hangterrasse bietet und von da über das Schrägdach der Stiege auf die große Dachterrasse führt. Eine simple Schachtel, perfekt für die Topografie moduliert: auf engstem Raum wird ein Maximum an horizontalen Flächen geschaffen mit gedeckten, abgeschirmten und exponierten Freiplätzen. Der Steilhang bleibt auf allen Ebenen spürbar, wird räumlich und visuell einbezogen und genützt. So wird das Problem zum Potenzial gewendet.

Section and views; carcass; CAD perspective; construction
Schnitt und Ansichten; Rohbau; CAD-Perspektive; Ausführung

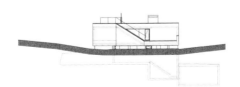

urbanity

is

Reduced 2 The Max
reduced 2 the max

turn0n is AWG's internationally most commented and recognized project and – unlike their other concepts – is no immediately practicable answer to tricky situations. turn0n, in many ways euphorically and uncritically misunderstood, must rather be seen as a provocative, almost caricatured statement on current residential philosophies. Once again, the model of automobile business is demonstrated to the building and furniture industry and its potential projected into a further techno-vision of housing – tracking the relevant trail of astronauts' capsules and the tubular prototypes for synthetic and automatic dwelling caves designed from the 50s to the 60s. What AWG primarily communicates is an impetus to reform building industries and architects' corresponding approach to design. Their impact is a much more powerful meshwork of planning teams and constructional components from which no call is heard for creative individuality, quite like in the case of automobile or EDP combines. Rather, functional and technical optimization would be essential with a teamwork objective to mass-produce ever smaller, ever more powerful components that at once facilitate ever larger ranges of individual operational freedom for end users.

turn0n ist das bisher am meisten beachtete, international kommentierte Projekt von AWG, ist aber – anders als ihre sonstigen Konzepte – keine sofort praktikable Antwort auf vertrackte Situationen. Vielfach euphorisch unkritisch missverstanden, ist turn0n eher als provokantes, fast karikaturhaftes Statement zu aktuellen Wohnphilosophien zu sehen. Einmal mehr wird damit der Bau- und Einrichtungsindustrie das Vorbild der Automobilbranche vorgeführt und deren Potenziale in eine weitere Techno-Wohnvision projiziert – auf den einschlägigen Spuren der Astronauten-Kapseln und der röhrenförmigen Prototypen für Kunst-stoff- und Automaten-Wohnhöhlen aus den fünfziger und sechziger Jahren. Was AWG damit aber primär kommuniziert, ist ein Anstoß zur Reform der Bauindustrien und auch der entsprechenden Entwurfs-haltung von Architekten – in Richtung einer viel stärkeren Netzwerk-bildung von Planungsteams und Baukomponenten, wo analog zu den Automobil- oder EDV-Konzernen nicht gestalterische Individualität gefragt ist, sondern die funktionelle und technische Optimierung im Teamwork zur Massenproduktion von letztlich immer kleineren, immer leistungsfähigeren Komponenten, die zugleich immer größere Bandbreiten individueller Nutzungsfreiheit für die Endverbraucher eröffnen.

Prototype, k/haus, Vienna, 2000; generation, addition of module
Prototyp, k/haus Wien; Generierung, Addition des Moduls

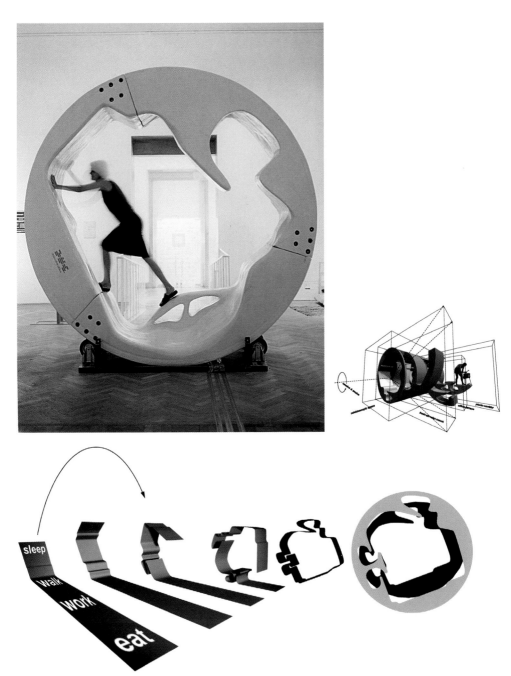

Densification, No Divestiture
Verdichtung statt Entflechtung

Three superregional routes of transportation run through the urban space: the existing railway route, chiefly used for passenger services, the planned railway route to serve as key north-south freight traffic connection, and the Brenner highway. The project develops an offensive superstructural and connecting strategy for all traffic networks. The infrastructure and city are not separated, but rather integrated such that synergy results from the two systems. Along the railway bridge over the Eisack, the speedway crossing 8 m above will be widened to form a freely passable surface. Linking the highway, the speedway and local roads, the bridge communicates with the railroad freight route via large loading docks. This serves to make the fallows along the southern junction available for a logistics center, terminals and services located directly at the existing industrial zone. The area of the railroad station is modified such that the existing barriers to the old town are neutralized and the fallows become an urban extension. The new railroad route is integrated in heterogeneously serviceable superstructures. At the central Virgl viaduct arching over the highway, likewise, the adjacent railroad route will be interpreted in terms of creating a complex traffic and urban junction to show the highest possible frequency of passers-by: street junctions turn into attractive superstructures, and downtown complexes are opened to traffic.

Drei überregionale Verkehrsträger durchziehen den Stadtraum: die bestehende Eisenbahntrasse, primär für Personenverkehr, die geplante Hochleistungstrasse der Bahn als wichtigste Nord-Süd-Verbindung für Gütertransport und die Brenner-Autobahn. Das Projekt bringt als Alternative zur geplanten Bypass-Trasse eine offensive Überbauungs- und Verknüpfungsstrategie aller Verkehrsnetze. Infrastruktur und Stadt werden nicht entflochten, sondern integriert, sodass eine Synergie beider Systeme entsteht. An der Bahnbrücke über den Eisack wird die in 8 m Höhe querende Schnellstraße zu einer frei befahrbaren Oberfläche verbreitert. Sie verbindet Autobahn, Schnellstraße sowie Lokalstraßen und wird über große Ladelifte mit der Gütertrasse der Bahn verbunden. So werden die Brachen am Süd-Knoten nutzbar für Logistikzentrum, Terminals und Servicedienste direkt an der bestehenden Industriezone. Das Bahnhofsareal wird so modifiziert, dass die existierenden Barrieren zur Altstadt fallen und die Brachen hier zur City-Erweiterung werden können. Die neue Bahntrasse wird in heterogen nutzbare Überbauungen integriert. Auch am zentralen Virgl-Viadukt der Autobahn wird die herangeführte Bahntrasse zur Schaffung eines komplexen Verkehrs- und Stadtknotens mit dichtester Passantenfrequenz interpretiert: Straßenknoten verwandeln sich in attraktive Überbauungen, citynahe Baukomplexe werden befahr- und durchfahrbar.

Diagrams and model: route superstructure
Diagramme und Modell: Überbauung Verkehrstrasse

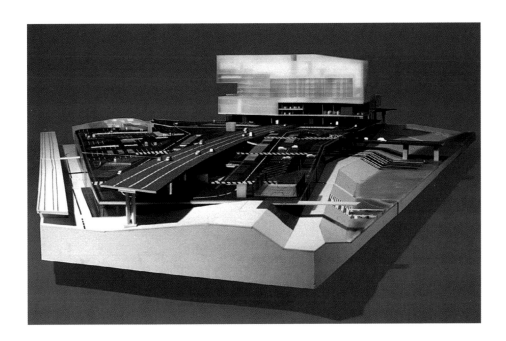

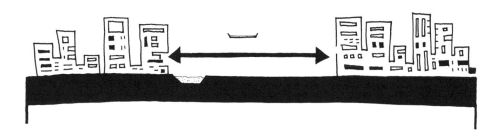

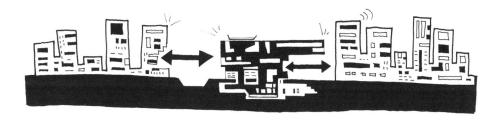

z.B. BZ., Urbanistic Study
Städtebauliche Studie

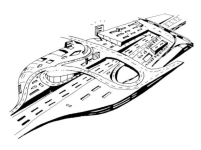

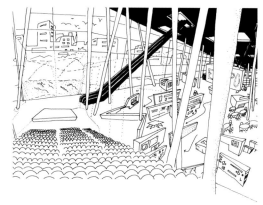

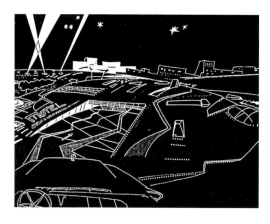

Visions of urbanized routes
Visionen zur Urbanisierung von Verkehrstrassen

AllesWirdGut
Große Neugasse 27, A–1040 Wien
Tel +43-1-961 04 37, Fax +43-1-961 03 11
awg@alleswirdgut.cc, www.alleswirdgut.cc

Ingrid Hora *76, **Andreas Marth** *69, **Friedrich Passler** *69, **Herwig Spiegl** *73, **Christian Waldner** *71, have been working together, as AllesWirdGut since 1999, on projects of various scales – including urbanistic strategies, interior work and design; drive a Mercedes 230CE/82; go to the Schikaneder, Shamrock and expedit; enjoy Fridge, Motorpsycho, Beck, Cabaret Voltaire, Madonna and Guy Ritchie (alright: George Clooney, too).
Buildings, projects (select): DOZ, DOrfZentrum, Multipurpose Building, Fließ, Tirol, competition, 1999–2001; FUZI, Free-Space Planning (1st phase), Innichen/San Candido, South Tirol, competition, 1999–2002 ; turn0n, housing vision, everywhere & nowhere, 2000; DONG, Conversion of DON GIL Shops, Graz, Styria, and Pasching, Upper Austria, 2000ff; HIM Shop Conversion, Innichen, South Tirol, 2001; MBM Single-Family Dwelling, Fließ, Tirol, 2001–02; mq 21, Interior Work, MuseumsQuartier Wien, 2001–02. Planned / under construction: SI+, Single-Family Dwelling (together with Rainer Pirker ARCHItexture team and werkraum), Vienna; geo, Factory Building, South Tirol; FUZI (2nd phase).

Ingrid Hora *76, **Andreas Marth** *69, **Friedrich Passler** *69, **Herwig Spiegl** *73, **Christian Waldner** *71, arbeiten seit 1999 als AllesWirdGut an Projekten unterschiedlichen Maßstabs – von Städtebau-strategien bis zu Innenraumgestaltung und Design – zusammen, fahren Mercedes 230CE, BJ 82, gehen ins Schikaneder, Shamrock, expedit, mögen Fridge, Motorpsycho, Beck, Cabaret Voltaire, Madonna und Guy Ritchie (okay, auch George Clooney).
Bauten, Projekte (Auswahl): 1999–2001 DOZ, DOrfZentrum, Mehr-zweckgebäude, Fließ, Tirol, Wettbewerb; 1999–2002 FUZI, Freiraum-planung (1.Phase), Innichen/San Candido, Südtirol, Wettbewerb; 2000 turn0n, wohnvision, überall & nirgends; seit 2000 DONG, Umbau DON GIL Shops, Graz, Steiermark, und Pasching, OÖ; 2001 HIM Geschäftsumbau, Innichen, Südtirol; 2001–02 MBM Einfamilienhaus, Fließ, Tirol; 2001–02 mq21, Innenausbau, MuseumsQuartier Wien.
In Planung/Bau: SI+, Einfamilienhaus (mit Rainer Pirker ARCHItexture team und werkraum), Wien; geo, Betriebsgebäude, Südtirol; FUZI (2.Phase).

DONG (DON GIL Shop Design)
DONG #10, competition / Wettbewerb, Graz
Project partner / Projektpartner: BSW19
Client / Bauherr: DON GIL Textilhandels AG
Collaborators / Mitarbeiterinnen: Erika Ratavay, Nadine Berger
Statics / Statik: Kaufmann Kriebernegg
Lighting consultant / Lichtkonsulent: Christian Ploderer
DONG #12, Pasching
Project partner / Projektpartner: BSW19
Client / Bauherr: DON GIL Textilhandels AG
Collaborator / Mitarbeiter: Matthias Raiger

FUZI, Free-Space Planning (1ˢᵗ phase), competition / Freiraumplanung (1. Phase), Wettbewerb,
Innichen / San Candido
Client / Bauherr: Municipality / Gemeinde Innichen
Collaborators / Mitarbeiter: Sebastian Gretzer, Gilles Delalex
Consultants / Konsulenten: Konzept Licht Steindl

DOZ, DOrfZentrum, Multipurpose Building, competition / Mehrzweckgebäude, Wettbewerb, Fließ
Client / Bauherr: Municipality / Gemeinde Fließ
Collaborator / Mitarbeiter: Herwig Göbel
Statics / Statik: Georg Pfenninger
Local supervision / Örtliche Bauaufsicht: Karl Gitterle

MBM, Single-Family Dwelling / Einfamilienhaus, Fließ
Client / Bauherr: B.+M. Wohlfarter
Collaborator / Mitarbeiter: Peter Döllmann
Statics / Statik: Werner Zanon

turn0n, housing vision, everywhere & nowhere / wohnvision, überall & nirgends
Project partner / Projektpartner: Tischlerei Franz Walder GesmbH

z. B. BZ., Urbanistic Study / Städtebauliche Studie, Bolzano/Bozen

With the kind support of / Mit freundlicher Unterstützung von:
WALDER FRANZ GMBH
Werkstätte für Raumgestaltung
A–9931 Ausservillgraten Nr. 42
walder.tischlerei@utanet.at

Architekturzentrum Wien; Springer-Verlag Wien New York; Text: © Otto Kapfinger

Photo credits: © by the architects and: Michael Dürr: 31; Hertha Hurnaus: 13, 15, 17, 19–21, 23–27

Feyferlik / Fritzer

Expressiveness is not their cup of tea, nor is a form that would 'blast' borders. Wolfgang Feyferlik's early work and that developed with Susi Fritzer together represent a 'bodiless architecture'. They employ the material features of structures and envelopes as discretely, as porously as possible, in an attempt to unfold a spatial totality, organized in a way that is not burdened by materiality. Feyferlik once announced a vision to 'build up a magnetic field that does no harm to people and at once separates cold and warm areas, such that an envelope is created with that magnetic field alone, corresponding to the people's requirements for comfort.' This premise makes it clear how he, together with Fritzer, aspires to a minimum of material efforts to create the psycho-physiological requirements of dwellings. Contrary to classic modernity, the material is not abstracted; all building materials are applied and exploited according to their performance properties, their potentials tested with perfect ease. Moreover, the spatial continuum in Feyferlik / Fritzer's concept is not only horizontally isotropic, such as with Mies van der Rohe who formulated open space as sandwiched between a podium and abstractly floating roofing panels. It is neither reminiscent of the tridimensional heterotopia associated with Van Doesburg's surface composition, nor is it a morphed atopy of an advanced membrane technique. Lacking pathos, the relaxed transparency in Feyferlik / Fritzer

Relaxed Without Limits
Entspannt grenzenlos

Expression ist nicht ihre Sache, nicht die Grenzen ‚sprengende' Form. Die frühen Bauten von Wolfgang Feyferlik und die nun in Partnerschaft mit Susi Fritzer entstandenen bilden eine ‚körperlose Architektur'. Sie benutzen das Stoffliche von Struktur und Hülle so diskret, so porös wie möglich, um die vom Stofflichen unbeschwert organisierte Entfaltung räumlicher Totalität zu erreichen. Feyferlik nannte als Vision einmal die Möglichkeit, ‚ein Magnetfeld aufzubauen, das dem Menschen nicht schadet und gleichzeitig eine Trennung zwischen kaltem und warmem Bereich ergibt, dass also allein durch das Magnetfeld eine Hülle geschaffen wird, die dem behaglichen Bedürfnis des Menschen entspricht'. Unter dieser Prämisse wird deutlich, wie er, mit Fritzer, ein Minimum an materiellem Einsatz anstrebt, um die psycho-physiologischen Anforderungen von Behausungen herzustellen. Anders als in der klassischen Moderne wird das Material nicht abstrahiert; jeder Baustoff wird seinem Leistungsprofil gemäß eingesetzt und ausgereizt, spielerisch in seinen Potenzialen erprobt. Überdies ist das Raumkontinuum im Konzept von Feyferlik / Fritzer nicht bloß horizontal isotrop, wie etwa bei Mies van der Rohe, der den offenen Raum als Sandwich zwischen einem Podium und abstrakt schwebenden Dachplatten formulierte. Noch ist es die dreidimensionale Heterotopie Van Doesburgscher Flächenkomposition, noch ist es gemorphte Atopie avancierter Mem-

St. House, Tainach, 1992; minimal apartment, collector façade
Minimalwohnung, Kollektorfassade

develops from simple layers and surfaces. Their choreography and differentiation allow diversely dosed penetrations from within and without to run along all three spatial axes. The transitory moment is not exhausted with an inclination for maximal glass. Rather, all transitions, changing materials and spatial joints are carefully processed in order to functionally and formally activate openness, tension, lightness and 'fluidity'. No sculptural walls arrest the flow of light and space, not even in introverted areas. Every enveloping surface, horizontal or vertical, lucid or opaque, is interpreted unlimitedly, not in terms of 'endless' but accompanied by a tendency of lifted borders; even massive parts are thought as covers – shimmery, sheltering, but never hermetic. Feyferlik / Fritzer have been going their own way in the Graz scene. They are seldom present in the media, probably also because this architecture fails to give spectacular photography: it is explicitly conceived as an outward filter, an instrument of an immaterial atmosphere. The trilogy of art gallery projects for Graz, Bolzano and Brisbane demonstrates how such bearing carries on through small and large scales alike: impressive statements regarding the diffusion of urban space, traffic space and cultural spaces.

brantechnik. Die entspannte, unpathetische Transparenz bei Feyferlik / Fritzer entsteht aus einfachen Schichten und Flächen. Diese sind so choreografiert und differenziert, dass eine vielfältig dosierte Durchdringung von innen und außen in allen drei Raumachsen eintritt. Das transitorische Moment erschöpft sich nicht in der Tendenz zu maximalem Glas, vielmehr werden Übergänge, Materialwechsel und Raumgelenke sorgfältig bearbeitet, um Offenheit, Spannung, Leichtigkeit und ‚Flüssigkeit' funktionell und formal zu aktivieren. Nirgendwo, auch in introvertierten Bereichen, soll der Fluss von Licht und Raum durch massiv-skulpturale Wände gebrochen werden. Jede Hüllfläche, horizontal oder vertikal, luzid oder opak, ist grenzenlos aufgefasst, nicht im Sinn von ‚endlos', sondern mit der Tendenz des Aufhebens von Grenzen; selbst massive Teile sind als Paravents gedacht: schirmend, bergend, nie aber hermetisch. In der Grazer Szene gehen Feyferlik / Fritzer eigene Wege, medial wenig präsent, wohl auch deshalb, weil diese Architektur keine spektakulären Fotos von sich selbst liefert, ist sie doch explizit als Filter nach Draußen konzipiert, als Instrument immaterieller Atmosphäre. Dass diese Haltung vom kleinen bis zum großen Maßstab durchträgt, zeigt die Trilogie der Kunsthausprojekte für Graz, Bozen und Brisbane: beeindruckende Statements der Diffusion von Stadtraum, Verkehrsraum und Kulturräumen.

Practice, 1994, lightweight well into the furniture's details
Dr. Doppelhofers Praxis, Leichtbau bis ins Möbeldetail

Art Space is Urban Space
Kunstraum ist Stadtraum

Future art galleries will offer open, flexible spatial structures that are closely interlaced with urban spaces. The flows of motion and lingering zones associated with pedestrians, automobiles and other media of transportation will be brought up to and lead through art spaces from attractively applied free spaces with graded accesses. This is the key message emerging from several competition contributions that Feyferlik/ Fritzer developed for international contexts. In the Kunsthaus Graz, they took a risk and brilliantly disregarded the invitation to tender, swiveling the street from the riverside into the property and thus achieving an open and intensive intertwinement of all ratios of space and traffic underneath the new art gallery: a singular, much-renowned approach. The circumstances were similar in Brisbane. The Queensland Gallery of Modern Art was to be developed between a main street and the riverbank. Here, the site descending to the river was conceived as an artificial landscape, equipped with ramps and plateaus and structured by the floating gallery's 'forest of columns'; a restaurant, lobby and groups of elevators form 'islands' on this 'plaza', linking the service areas inserted below into the slope with garages, studios and the art gallery's conch that is open upwards – a peripherally passable terrace space, roofed by a luminous ceiling with a membrane skin.

Die Kunsthäuser der Zukunft werden offene, flexible Raumstrukturen anbieten, in enger Verflechtung mit urbanen Räumen. Die Bewegungsströme und Verweilzonen von Fußgängern, PKWs und anderen Transportmedien werden aus attraktiv instrumentierten Freiflächen mit gestaffelten Zugängen an die Kunsträume heran und durch sie hindurchführen. Dies ist die Kernaussage einiger Wettbewerbsbeiträge, die Feyferlik/Fritzer für internationale Kontexte entwickelten. Beim Kunsthaus Graz setzten sie sich riskant, doch brillant über die Ausschreibung hinweg, verschwenkten die Straße vom Flussufer ins Grundstück und erreichten damit eine offene, intensive Verflechtung aller Raum- und Verkehrsrelationen unter dem neuen Kunsthaus: ein singulärer, vielbeachteter Ansatz. In Brisbane war die Lage ähnlich. Die Queensland Gallery of Modern Art soll zwischen einer Hauptstraße und dem Flussufer entstehen. Hier ist das zum Ufer abfallende Gelände als künstliche Landschaft gedacht, versehen mit Rampen und Plateaus, strukturiert durch den ‚Stützenwald‘ der schwebenden Kunsthalle; Restaurant, Foyer und Liftgruppen bilden ‚Inseln‘ auf dieser ‚Plaza‘, verbinden die in den Hang darunter eingeschobenen Serviceflächen, Garagen und Ateliers mit der nach oben offenen Muschel der Kunsthalle – ein peripher durchwanderbarer Terrassenraum, überdacht durch eine Lichtdecke mit Membranhaut.

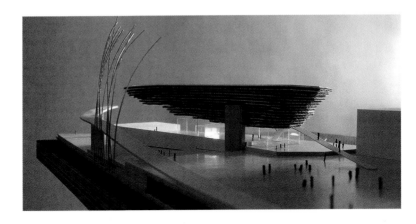

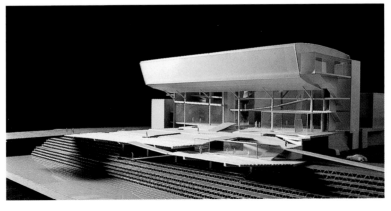

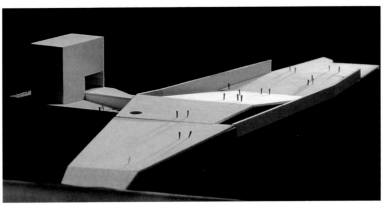

Kunsthaus Bozen; Kunsthaus Graz; Queensland Gallery; models
Modelle

Queensland Gallery of Modern Art, competition, Brisbane, 2001
Wettbewerb

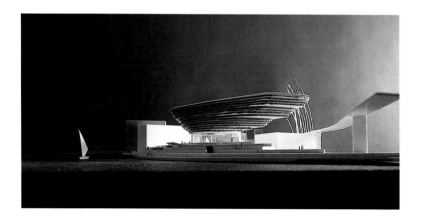

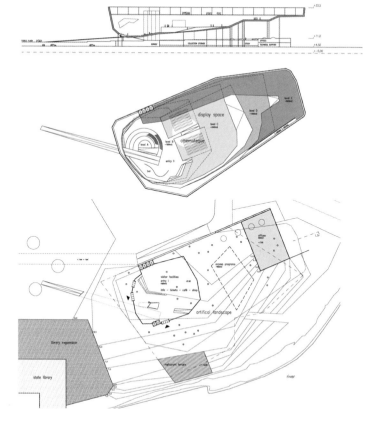

Ground plans, section, view of model
Grundrisse, Schnitt, Modellansicht

Spielfeld Veterinary Station and Customs Office, Reconstruction/Conversion, Styria, 1996–2000
Veterinär- und Zollstation Spielfeld, Neu-/Umbau

Thin Skin: Significance and Wit
Thin Skin: Sinn mit Witz

Conversions of and annexes to stations along the border of the European Union, to be removed once Slovenia joins the Union in several years time. The order was to be carried out with a minimal budget – a task that was accomplished without drawbacks on account of the architects taking over construction management and owing to genuine cooperation with the occupants. From the outset, furthermore, Feyferlik / Fritzer's competition project was oriented to an economical conception that elaborates the plant's transitory character in all respects. Set up first, the veterinary ward was given a steel framework with wall panels that change with the functional areas. The roof and walls are lined on the outside with high-tensile foil and guyed down with steel ropes. This innovation resulted in a façade price one third of the usual, without making use of attic details or eaves troughs. The skin is stretched back over the underside on the ramp's canopy: at night, the overhang with integrated lanterns becomes a body of light. The administration wing across is developed as a bridge under which was developed a roofed parking and service zone for trucks, communicating freely with the renovated old building. Wooden sandwich elements serve as a climatic envelope for the steel framework. Here as well, the outer skin of white foil is stretched all around, while rain is discharged through interior drainage.

Um- und Zubauten der Stationen an einer EU-Außengrenze, die in einigen Jahren durch den Beitritt Sloweniens fallen wird. Der Auftrag war mit minimalen Budgets durchzuführen, was mit der Bauleitung durch die Architekten und die gute Kooperation mit den Nutzern aber ohne Abstriche gelang. Überdies war das Wettbewerbsprojekt von Feyferlik / Fritzer von vornherein auf eine ökonomische Konzeption ausgerichtet, die den transitorischen Charakter der Anlage in jeder Hinsicht thematisiert. Die zuerst errichtete Veterinärstation hat ein Stahlfachwerk mit unterschiedlichen Wandpaneelen entsprechend den Funktionsbereichen. Dach und Wände sind außen fugenlos mit hochfester Folie überzogen, mit Stahlseilen nach unten abgespannt. Ohne Attikadetails und Dachrinnen konnte durch diese Innovation der Fassadenpreis auf ein Drittel des Üblichen gesenkt werden. Am Vordach der Rampe ist die Haut über die Unterseite zurückgespannt: mit integrierten Leuchten wird die Auskragung nachts zum Lichtkörper. Der Verwaltungstrakt gegenüber ist als Brücke ausgebildet, unter der ein gedeckter LKW-Park- und Abfertigungsplatz mit offener Kommunikation zum adaptierten Altbau entstand. Das Stahlfachwerk hat als Klimahülle Holz-Sandwichelemente. Auch hier ist als Außenhaut die weiße Folie über alles gespannt, der Regen aber über Innenentwässerung abgeleitet.

Veterinary station; total view with truck dispatch
Veterinärstation; Gesamtansicht mit LKW-Abfertigung

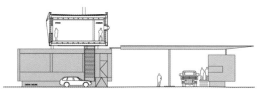

Administration wing, corridor; section; truck dispatch counter
Flur Verwaltungstrakt; Schnitt; Schalter LKW-Abfertigung

Veterinary Station; section
Veterinärstation; Schnitt

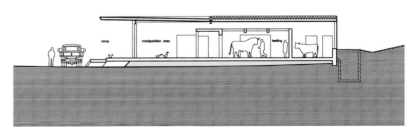

C. House, Graz, 1997–99
Haus C.

The property descends to the north and is lined on two sides by public pathways. Planned for a family of five, the building transforms the difficult topography into a habitable landscape, links an interior openness with the pleasures of free spaces including a rooftop pool and solarium, shielded discreetly against exterior ways and arranged in a functionally flexible constellation. The house is set close to an immense avenue on the lowest point of the area. At ground level, the elevated main story results in an informal, covered zone accommodating storage, commercial and playing areas, as well as a paned lobby. Above, a large spatial continuum flowing outward to the south is clearly marked off to the north and against insights from the pathways. Here, the supporting and screening concrete structure is spanned with a protective skin of black sheets, underlining and modifying the elevated section's partial hermetism. Seamlessly elegant, the section is barely visible beside the trees, but also appears absolutely light and ephemeral. All elements and details are worked with the same unspectaculary artfulness. Precise functionality is refined, increased to a subliminal sensuality. The kids' area is located beneath the terrace's western part and can also be used separately or for different purposes.

Habitable Landscape
Bewohnbare Landschaft

Der Grund fällt nach Norden ab und wird an zwei Seiten von öffentlichen Wegen gesäumt. Für eine Familie mit drei Kindern geplant, transformiert der Bau die schwierige Topografie zu einer bewohnbaren Landschaft, verbindet innere Offenheit, Genuss der Freiräume samt Pool und Solarium am Dach mit dezenter Abschirmung gegen die äußeren Wege und mit einer funktionell flexiblen Konstellation. Am untersten Punkt des Geländes ist das Haus knapp an die mächtige Allee gesetzt. Das Aufständern der Hauptebene ergibt ebenerdig die informelle, gedeckte Zone für Lager-, Wirtschafts-, Spielbereiche und das verglaste Foyer. Darüber liegt ein nach Süden von innen nach außen fließendes, großes Raumkontinuum, das sich klar gegen Norden und die Einsicht von den Wegen abgrenzt. Die tragende und schirmende Betonstruktur ist hier mit einer Schutzhaut aus schwarzer Folie überspannt. Sie unterstreicht und relativiert zugleich die partielle Hermetik des aufgeständerten Trakts. Mit fugenloser Eleganz ist er neben den Bäumen fast unsichtbar, wirkt aber auch absolut leicht und ephemer. Mit derselben unspektakulären Raffinesse sind sämtliche Elemente und Details durchgestaltet. Präzise Funktionalität ist da zur unterschwelligen Sinnlichkeit verfeinert, gesteigert. Der Kinderbereich liegt unter dem Westteil der Terrasse und kann auch separat oder anders genutzt werden.

View from the children's section to the lobby and the upper level
Blick vom Kindertrakt zum Foyer und zum Obergeschoß

C. House
Haus C.

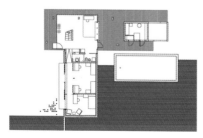

R. House, Graz, 2000–02
Haus R.

Kitchen area, southeastern view; view southwestern terrace
Küchenbereich, Blick nach SO; Ansicht SW-Terrasse

R. House
Haus R.

Transformed Landscape
Transformierte Landschaft

The building concept elevates the location's qualities to a scene. The functions are divided into individual bodies, and these are inserted into the topography such that manifold new spaces develop between architecture and nature – beyond any linear diffusion. Dropping to the east, the sloped allotment is a square in a ratio of 1:2, screwed out lengthwise to the southeast by some 30°. The access is located on the narrow side. A carport leads to the entrance on the property's southern corner. A body shell cut into the site first blocks views to the house – no gatehouse, but a broadly paned sound studio that opens to the north under a roofing panel that projects over the carport and hallway. The access to the dwelling leads through a grove up to the higher part of the area, to meet the heart of a long-drawn mellow figure fit in between and under the broad-leaved trees. The residential area is furnished with glass panes that are shaded by the trees. It looks out to the southeast and southwest and also receives top light from the roof on its northern corner. The kitchen along the inclined glazing enjoys a 120° panorama. A wooden box, the parents' bedroom area adjoins in the corner and marks a turning point in front of the building's northern corner. It detaches itself from the ground and lifts the children's area, another box, into the treetops where the kids can break cover on a roof terrace above the low lobby.

Das Baukonzept steigert die Qualitäten des Ortes zur Szene. Die Funktionen sind in Einzelkörper zerteilt und diese sind so ins Terrain gesetzt, dass zwischen Architektur und Natur – über die lineare Diffusion hinaus – vielfältige neue Räume entstehen. Der Hang fällt nach Osten, die Parzelle ist ein Rechteck im Verhältnis 1:2, in der Längsrichtung um gut 30° nach Südosten herausgedreht. An der Schmalseite liegt die Zufahrt. Ein Carport leitet zum Eingang an der Süd-Ecke des Grundstücks. Den Blick zum Haus blockiert zunächst ein ins Gelände geschnittener Baukörper, kein Pförtnerhaus, sondern ein Tonstudio, das sich mit breiter Verglasung nach Norden öffnet. Der Zugang zum Wohnhaus führt von unten durch eine lichte Baumgruppe hindurch zum höheren Bereich des Areals und trifft auf den Angelpunkt einer langgestreckten, aufgelockerten Baufigur, die hier zwischen und unter die Laubbäume eingepasst ist. Der Wohnbereich blickt mit von Bäumen beschatteten Glasflächen nach Südost und Südwest, erhält auch Oberlicht vom Dach an seiner Nord-Ecke. Die Küche entlang der Schrägverglasung hat ein 120° Panorama. Der Elternschlafteil schließt im Winkel als hölzerne Box an und bildet eine Zäsur vor dem Nordende des Gebäudes, wo es sich vom Boden löst und eine weitere Box als Kinderbereich in die Baumkronen hebt, mit Austritt auf eine Dachterrasse über dem niedrig gehaltenen Foyer.

Ground plan; wooden box parents' area; view to the studio
Grundriss; Holzbox Elternteil; Blick zum Studio

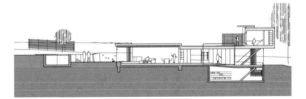

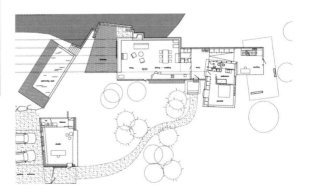

Architecture as a Time Store
Baukunst als Zeitspeicher

The Mariazell basilica and clerical house are marked by many centuries of building layers. Saturated, or even burdened, as the most significant place of pilgrimage in present-day Austria and the old imperial and royal monarchy, interventions of a sophisticated modernity were somewhat unexpected, not to say: sensational. Planning will have been developed and materialized over a period of 15 years, a careful dialogue between the designers and the Benedictine Superior (of Mariazell) as client. Feyferlik/Fritzer generally argue in favor of slow conversions, they see a decisive moment in final reactions on site – provided the architect's competence and sufficient quality on the part of local craftsmen. This attitude allows to exceed prefab instant solutions in an individualizing and harmonizing endeavor. Also, the building sponsorship may grow along with the building process. 'Kill speed' would be the devise to grant planners and clients the adventure of building, fundamental at all times, and bridging concepts, materialization and occupational routine. The new popular altar and the membranous case given to the new organ are convincing elements in the basilica, as much as the new shrine equipped with a floating steel girder screen in the south tower, and the implanted superior's office, gallery and archive in the clerical house.

Basilika und Geistliches Haus von Mariazell sind geprägt durch Bauschichten vieler Jahrhunderte. Als bedeutendste Wallfahrtsstätte Österreichs und der alten k.u.k. Monarchie mit Traditionen gesättigt bzw. belastet, waren hier Interventionen anspruchsvoller Modernität zuletzt eher unerwartet, um nicht zu sagen: sensationell. Die Planung konnte in einem auf 15 Jahre angelegten Zeitraum entwickelt und umgesetzt werden, als sorgfältiger Dialog zwischen den Gestaltern und dem Benediktiner Superior (von Mariazell) als Bauherrn. Feyferlik/Fritzer propagieren generell ein langsames Umsetzen, sie sehen im finalen Reagieren noch auf der Baustelle – Kompetenz des Architekten und die regional vorhandene Qualität von Professionisten vorausgesetzt – ein entscheidendes Moment. Es ermöglicht einerseits, über Prefab-Instant-Lösungen hinauszugelangen, zu individualisieren und abzustimmen, und andererseits kann so auch die Bauherrschaft im Bauprozess mitwachsen. ‚Kill speed' wäre die Devise, um Planer wie Bauherrn das jedesmal fundamentale Abenteuer des Bauvorgangs zuzubilligen, als Brücke zwischen Konzept, Materialisierung und Nutzungsalltag. In der Basilika überzeugen der neue Volksaltar und die membranhafte Fassung der neuen Orgel, im Südturm die neue Reliquienkammer mit schwebendem Stahltragrost, im Geistlichen Haus die implantierte Superioratskanzlei mit Galerie und Archiv.

New organ, popular altar in the basilica; shrine
Neue Orgel, Volksaltar in der Basilika; Reliquienkammer

Insert 'Bath-Tower', (guest)rooms; partial view superior's office, gallery
Einbau ‚Badturm', Gästetrakt; Teilansicht Superioratskanzlei, Galerie

Feyferlik / Fritzer
Glacisstraße 7, A–8010 Graz
Tel +43-316-34 76 56, Fax +43-316-38 60 29
feyferlik@inode.at, fritzer@inode.cc

Wolfgang Feyferlik, born in Hausham/D in 1957; studied architecture at Graz TU.
Buildings, projects (select): 'Solo' Housing Estate, Deutschlandsberg (competition 1st prize, together with Hubert Wolfschwenger), 1983–93. 1983–94: various houses (Graz, St. Anna, Vienna, etc.), and competitions (e.g. in Austria and Spain).
Susi Fritzer, born in Graz/A in 1967; studied architecture at Graz TU and at the Städelschule in Frankfurt.
Buildings, projects (select): Europan 4, Palma de Mallorca, competition (2nd prize), 1997; Aachen Institute of Technology Students Center, competition (1st prize, together with Eva-Maria Pape), 2000. Collaboration since 1994.
Joint buildings, projects (select): Basilica and Clerical House, Reorganization and Reconstructions, Mariazell, Styria, 1992–2007; Augarten Footbridge, competition, Graz, 1996; C. House, Graz, 1997–99; Graz Town Hall, competition (purchase), 1999; Kunsthaus Graz, competition (purchase), 2000; Dr. D.'s Apartment, Vienna, 2001; Queensland Gallery of Modern Art, competition, Brisbane, 2001; R. House, Graz, 2000–02.

Wolfgang Feyferlik, geboren 1957 Hausham, Deutschland; Architekturstudium TU Graz.
Bauten, Projekte (Auswahl): 1983–93 Wohnbau ‚Solo‘, Deutschlandsberg (Wettbewerb, 1. Preis, mit Hubert Wolfschwenger). 1983–94: Diverse Häuser (Graz, St. Anna, Wien etc.) und Wettbewerbe (z. B. in Österreich und Spanien).
Susi Fritzer, geboren 1967 Graz; Architekturstudium TU Graz, Städelschule Frankfurt/Main.
Bauten, Projekte (Auswahl): 1997 Europan 4, Palma de Mallorca, Wettbewerb (2. Preis); 2000 Studienfunktionales Zentrum der RWTH Aachen, Wettbewerb (1. Preis, mit Eva-Maria Pape).
Zusammenarbeit seit 1994.
Gemeinsame Bauten, Projekte (Auswahl): 1992–2007 Basilika und Geistliches Haus, Neugestaltung und Umbauten, Mariazell, Steiermark. 1996 Augartensteg, Wettbewerb; 1997–99 Haus C.; 1999 Stadthalle Graz, Wettbewerb (Ankauf); 2000 Kunsthaus Graz, Wettbewerb (Ankauf); alle Graz. 2001 Wohnung Dr. D., Wien; 2001 Queensland Gallery of Modern Art, Wettbewerb, Brisbane; 2000–02 Haus R., Graz.

St. House / Haus St., Tainach
Client / Bauherr: Familie St.
Statics / Statik: DI Alois Winkler

Dr. Doppelhofer's Practice / Praxis Dr. Doppelhofer, Neudau
Client / Bauherr: Dr. Elke and/und Dr. Hans Doppelhofer
Collaborators / Mitarbeiter: Fritz Mooshammer, Alfred Resch, Birgit Rudacs
Statics / Statik: DI Alois Winkler

Kunsthaus Graz, competition, purchase / Kunsthaus Graz, Wettbewerb, Ankauf
Promoter / Auslober: City of Graz / Stadt Graz
Collaborators / Mitarbeiter: Harald Kloiber, Hubert Schuller (model / Modell),
Paul Ott (photos / Fotos)
Statics / Statik: DI Alois Winkler (consultation / Beratung)

Kunsthaus Bozen, competition / Kunsthaus Bozen, Wettbewerb
Project partner / Projektpartner: Arch. Georg Giebeler, Köln
Promoter / Auslober: City of Bolzano / Stadt Bozen
Collaborators / Mitarbeiter: Jürgen Roegener, Hubert Schuller (model / Modell), Paul Ott
(photos / Fotos)

Queensland Gallery of Modern Art, competition / Queensland Gallery of Modern Art,
Wettbewerb, Brisbane
Promoter / Auslober: Government of Queensland
Collaborators / Mitarbeiter: Harald Kloiber, Hubert Schuller (model / Modell),
Paul Ott (photos / Fotos)

Veterinary Station and Customs Office, Reconstruction/Conversion, competition 1st prize /
Veterinär- und Zollstation, Neu-/Umbau, Wettbewerb, 1. Preis, Spielfeld
Client / Bauherr: Republic of Austria / Republik Österreich
Collaborators / Mitarbeiter: Birgit Wemmers, Patrick Überbacher
Statics / Statik: DI Alois Winkler
Electrical planning / Elektroplanung: Ing. Erwin Rauch

C. House / Haus C., Graz
Client / Bauherr: Familie C.
Collaborators / Mitarbeiter: Birgit Rudacs, Patrick Überbacher
Statics / Statik: DI Alois Winkler
Engineering of services / Haustechnik: Ing. Georg Kolb
Electrical planning / Elektroplanung: Ing. Erwin Rauch

R. House / Haus R., Graz
Client / Bauherr: Familie R.
Statics / Statik: DI Siegfried Hiebl

Basilica and Clerical House, Reorganization and Reconstructions / Basilika und Geistliches
Haus, Neugestaltung und Umbauten, Mariazell
Project partner / Projektpartner: Arch. Georg Giebeler, Köln
Client / Bauherr: Benediktiner Superiorat Mariazell
Project coordination / Projektkoordinator: BM Anton Nolz
Collaborators / Mitarbeiter: Berthold Henzler, Jürgen Roegener
Statics / Statik: DI Herbert Majcenovic
Engineering of services / Haustechnik: Ing. Georg Kolb
Electrical planning / Elektroplanung: DI Oswald Petschenig

Architekturzentrum Wien; Springer-Verlag Wien New York; Text: © Otto Kapfinger
Photo credits: © by the architects and: Paul Ott: 37, 39, 41, 43–45, 47–49, 52, 53, 55, 57, 58; Ralph
Richter: 51, 52

Holz Box Tirol

Their office is a roof extension in downtown Innsbruck: utmost use of space with prefab elements and a minimum of lost pathways under a straitjacketing steep roof form that could not be changed. Extreme values of economy are achieved in the toilet cell and in the Minibox fixed to the elevator annex as a meeting room. In view of 60 cm of width given to the WC, practically and laconically mastered down to the last detail, it becomes clear to any visitor: these architects are different from the 'autochthonous' Tirolians. Erich Strolz and Armin Kathan were bred on the Vorarlberg side of the Arlberg mountain. Strolz originates in the Hochtannberg Pass at Warth; his first building, in 1992, was a personnel section for the Adler Hotel in Hochkrumbach situated at a height of 1600 m where winters last for up to eight months a year, where meters high snowdrifts and horizontal (!) snow- and rainfalls are part of everyday life. Loveliness or expressiveness rendered to constructions are out of place here, unlike robustness, extreme compactness of volumes, and a perfect interior economy. Armin Kathan comes from Lech at a height of 1500 m, also built by Walsers whose rigid mentality is still perceptible in a commercial respect. Kathan's inaugural building was an extension for the Rote Wand Hotel in Lech-Zug in 1989. His unspectacular attempt to break through the cliché of a prevalent lederhosen style and to further develop the inner values, not the imported alienated

Ihr Büro ist ein Dachausbau im Stadtkern von Innsbruck: maximale Raumausnutzung mit vorgefertigten Elementen bei minimalen Verlusten an Wegflächen innerhalb der Zwangsjacke einer Steildachform, die nicht verändert werden konnte. Extremwerte der Ökonomie werden in der WC-Zelle und in der am Liftzubau als Sozialraum montierten Minibox erreicht. Bei 60 cm WC-Breite, die bis ins kleinste Detail praktisch und formal lakonisch beherrscht ist, wird wohl jedem Besucher klar: diese Architekten sind anders als die ‚autochthonen' Tiroler. Erich Strolz und Armin Kathan sind auf der Vorarlberger Seite des Arlbergs aufgewachsen. Strolz am Hochtannbergpass bei Warth; sein erster Bau war 1992 der Personaltrakt des Adler Hotels in Hochkrumbach auf 1600 m Höhe, wo bis zu acht Monate Winter herrscht, wo meterhohe Schneeverwehungen und waagrechte (!) Schnee- und Regenfälle zum Alltag gehören. Lieblichkeit oder Expressivität im Bauen ist hier fehl am Platz, dafür Robustheit, äußerste Kompaktheit der Volumina, perfekte Ökonomie im Innenraum. Armin Kathan stammt aus Lech, das auf 1500 m Höhe ebenfalls von Walsern gegründet wurde, deren rigide Mentalität in kommerzieller Hinsicht heute noch spürbar ist. Kathans erster Bau war 1989 eine Erweiterung zum Hotel Rote Wand in Lech-Zug. Sein unspektakulärer Versuch, die Klischees des gängigen Lederhosenstils zu durchbrechen und die inneren Werte, nicht die

Row Houses, Dwelling Box System, Sistrans
Reihenhausanlage, System Wohnbox

motives of Alpine building, caused much turmoil in the village, and the architect was forced to overcome downright existential attacks. In the 90s, Kathan, Strolz and the Holz Box Tirol team virtually imported the modern inclination for wooden structures flourishing in Vorarlberg to Tirol where a 'white' sculptural penmanship was predominant in solid construction as late as the 80s. In its geometrical bite, coarseness and angularity, the language used by Kathan & Strolz's constructions diverges from their Vorarlberg colleagues' currently more finely 'knit' minimalism. It is reminiscent of Albrecht's and Wäger's Minimal Houses from the 60s and the cheeky beginnings of the Cooperative Dornbirn. With the Holz Box Tirol prefab building system, in 1997/98, they transposed this unromantic, economic and environmental attitude held by Alpine building to the level of industrial production. As was once the case in the high-altitude regions, building on the outskirts of the present nomadic day is also oriented to minimizing all expenditures and a maximum of exposed life embedded in urbanistic surroundings. Holz Box Tirol offers no museum-piece architectural art, but fast, economy-priced, intelligent spatial systems, tools that are suited for everyday living and working.

importierten, verfremdeten Motive alpinen Bauens weiterzubilden, sorgte im Ort für gewaltigen Aufruhr, und der Architekt hatte handfeste, existenzbedrohende Attacken zu überstehen. Mit dem Team Holz Box Tirol haben Kathan & Strolz den in Vorarlberg florierenden Hang zum modernen Holzbau in den neunziger Jahren gleichsam nach Tirol importiert, wo ja noch in den achtziger Jahren eindeutig die ‚weiße‘, skulpturale Handschrift im Massivbau die Szene bestimmte. Die Sprache der Bauten von Kathan & Strolz unterscheidet sich in der geometrischen Schärfe, in der Rauheit und Kantigkeit von dem heute feiner ‚gestrickten‘ Minimalismus der Vorarlberger Kollegen, sie erinnert an die Minimalhäuser von Albrecht oder Wäger aus den sechziger Jahren und an die rotzigen Anfänge der Cooperative Dornbirn. Mit dem Fertigbausystem Holz Box Tirol transformierten sie 1997/98 diese unromantische, ökonomische und ökologische Haltung des alpinen Bauens auf die Ebene industrieller Produktion. Wie in den hohen Regionen einst ist auch das stadtperiphere Bauen der nomadischen Gegenwart auf Minimierung allen Aufwands und maximale Exponierung des Lebens im urbanistischen Umfeld ausgerichtet. Holz Box Tirol bietet nicht museumstaugliche Architekturkunst, sondern schnelle, preiswerte, intelligente Raumsysteme, alltagstaugliche Tools für heutiges Wohnen und Arbeiten.

Mpreis supermarket, Kematen, northern side
Lebensmittelmarkt Mpreis, Nordseite

bivouaks

In connection with the studio's roof enlargement, the team presents the minimum version of their multifaceted building set of modern timber materials. A cube with edges 2.6 m in length crowns the top of an elevator tower that has been newly set into the courtyard. The cube provides three to four sleeping places on two stories, a stove and cooking plate, dining room for four, a sanitary cell and storage space: 18 m³ of ingeniously usable space for the price of a subcompact, to be relished as a summerhouse, roof appurtenance, tree hut, bivouak hut, etc. The important point about this project is a wooden architecture reduced and transposed to a minimum of space, yet combined with supreme functionality. Particularly in terms of minimization, wood as a material can display its full qualities and neutralize the difference in scale between furniture and shells.

Wardrobe Trunk, Inhabitable
Schrankkoffer bewohnbar

Im Zusammenhang mit dem Dachausbau des Ateliers zeigt das Team die Minimalfassung ihres variantenreichen Baukastens aus modernen Holzwerkstoffen. Den im Hof neu angesetzten Aufzugsturm krönt ein Kubus von 2,6 m Kantenlänge. Er bietet drei bis vier Schlafplätze in zwei Etagen, Herd und Kochstelle, Essplatz für vier Personen, Sanitärzelle und Stauräume: 18 m³ ausgeklügelt nutzbarer Raum zum Preis eines Kleinwagens, brauchbar als Gartenhaus, Dachaufbau, Baumhaus, Biwakhütte etc. Der Clou dieses Projekts liegt in der Reduktion und Umsetzung von Holzarchitektur auf minimalen Raum bei maximaler Funktionalität. Gerade in der Minimierung kann der Werkstoff Holz alle seine Qualitäten voll ausspielen und die Maßstabsdifferenz zwischen Möbel und Gehäuse aufheben.

Holz Box Tirol

Section; stove-table combination, views
Schnitt; Kombination Herd und Tisch, Ansichten

Wooden Building in the System
Holzbau im System

Holz Box Tirol's system of prefab modules with low-energy values and solar energy supply remains the only one in Austria to be applied to detached houses, multistory row houses and terraced housing estates. The modules' ground plans measure 1.15 x 5.75 m; added eight times, a standard solution amounts to 50 m² furnished with a central core for stairway, sanitary and energy facilities. This set can be stacked up twice to three times. Organized concentrically, the rooms are neutral to occupancy, the façades freely formed, and longitudinal or cross-sectional additions can be implemented with terraces inserted in between. The construction consists of an interior structural system with metal columns and glulam girders that are set up in no time. The prefabricated ceilings and floors, the outer walls' wooden panels and the roof are fit and bolted into this structure. Complete bathrooms, kitchens and energy cords are integrated in plug-in, easily stacked cores. The outer walls are free of pipings, high-insulated, can be equipped with variable covering layers or solar panels, and be unscrewed, replaced or extended within the system, if required. A set of 100 m² is manufactured in three weeks, and is built on a baseplate in a day's work – a structure that is cheaper and more flexible than conventional ones.

Das von Holz Box Tirol entwickelte System vorgefertigter Module mit Niedrigenergiewerten und Solarversorgung ist in Österreich bisher das einzige, das sowohl für Einzelhäuser als auch für mehrgeschoßige Reihenhäuser und für Terrassensiedlungen zur Anwendung kam. Das Modul misst im Grundriss 1,15 x 5,75 m, achtmal addiert ergibt es eine Standardlösung von 50 m² mit einem zentralen Stiegen- und Sanitär- bzw. Energiekern. Dieses Set kann zwei- bis dreimal übereinandergestapelt werden. Die im Rundlauf organisierten Räume sind nutzungsneutral, die Fassaden frei gestaltbar, Additionen in Längs- oder Querrichtung sind mit zwischengeschalteten Terrassen durchführbar. Die Konstruktion besteht aus einem innenliegenden Tragsystem mit Metallstützen und Brettschichtträgern, die in kürzester Zeit montiert werden. In diese Struktur werden die vorgefertigten Decken samt Böden, die Holzpaneele der Außenwände und das Dach eingepasst und verschraubt. In den steck- und stapelbaren Kernen sind die kompletten Badezimmer, Küchen und Energiestränge integriert. Die Außenwände sind frei von Leitungen, hochgedämmt, können mit variablen Deckschichten oder Solarpaneelen ausgestattet und bei Bedarf abgeschraubt, ersetzt oder im System erweitert werden. Ein Set mit 100 m² wird in drei Wochen gefertigt, in einem Tag auf dem Fundament montiert, ist billiger und flexibler als konventionelle Bauten.

Building variants; prefab system, Row Houses, Sistrans
Bauvarianten; Prefab-System, Finish im Selbstbau; Reihenhäuser

39,0 M2 WNF   TYP 1   55,0 M2 WNF   TYP 2   71,0 M2 WNF   TYP 3   86,5 M2 WNF   TYP 4

Reasonable Densification
Verdichtung mit Verstand

The slope under the Innsbruck Nordkette is inclined on two sides. The plot is about 1000 m² large, the upper strip of which town planners had intended to use as an accessway and parking facilities. The location with a view on town is attractive, but for years was considered unsuitable for building purposes. The graded tower and terraced houses for a private building company contradicts two preconceptions: first, that 'prefab wooden boxes with low-energy values' inevitably result in spatial schematisms; and second, that architecture destroys the local slopes' topography. Strolz modified the Holz Box system according to the following criteria: a maximum of natural area preservation, the least possible intervention on the part of the houses into the ground, roofed parking along the road without the common shelter-like housing altogether counterbalancing the antagonism between densification and exposition to the valley view, between an optimal exterior orientation and protection of privacy. The four-story houses are shielded from one another by stairways, the transparency of which, however, allows for much direct and indirect light into the dark zones. The basement ventures into the open toward the west with French doors, thus allowing the 'cellars' to be adequately used. The main floors are closed in the front, open to the east and west with balconies and loggias. Small studios complement the phenomenal roof terraces.

Der Hang unter der Innsbrucker Nordkette ist nach zwei Seiten geneigt. Das Grundstück hat knapp 1000 m², wovon der obere Streifen von der Stadtplanung für Zufahrt und Parkierung gedacht war. Der Platz mit Blick über die Stadt ist attraktiv, galt aber jahrelang als unbebaubar. Die gestaffelten Turm-Terrassenhäuser für eine private Errichtergemeinschaft widerlegen zwei Vorurteile: dass ‚Prefab-Holz-Kisten mit Niedrigenergiewerten' zwangsläufig zu räumlichen Schematismen führen, und dass durch Bebauung die Topografie der lokalen Hänge zerstört wird. Strolz modifizierte das Holz-Box-System nach folgenden Kriterien: maximale Erhaltung des Naturgeländes, möglichst geringes Eindringen der Häuser ins Erdreich, gedeckte Parkierung an der Straße ohne die übliche, bunkerartige Einhausung; Ausgleich des Antagonismus zwischen Verdichtung und Exponierung zum Talblick, zwischen optimaler Orientierung nach außen und Sicherung der Privatheit. Die viergeschoßigen Häuser sind an der Bergseite durch die Stiegenhäuser voneinander abgeschirmt, durch deren Transparenz jedoch viel Licht direkt und indirekt in die Dunkelzonen kommt. Die Sockeletage geht nach Westen mit Fenstertüren ins Freie, so werden die ‚Keller' vollwertig nutzbar. Die Haupttetagen sind nach vorne geschlossen, öffnen sich nach Osten und Westen mit Balkonen und Loggien. Kleine Studios ergänzen die phänomenalen Dachterrassen.

Eastern view; view over town
Ostansicht; Blick über die Stadt

Holz Box Tirol

Jagdgasse Row Houses
Reihenhausanlage Jagdgasse

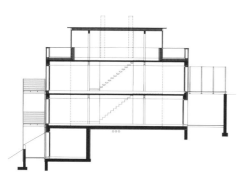

Section; eastern side with terraces, loggias; ground plan, interior, street side
Schnitt; Ostseite mit Terrassen, Loggien; Grundriss, Interieur, Straßenseite

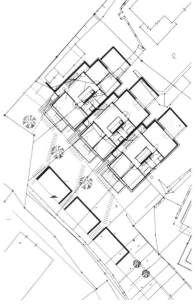

A demonstration of the versatility shown by the Holz Box system in a coupling of residential and working areas located on a northern slope. The precise and polar setting of two modular bodies remodels the property into an intense spatial figure. At the southern roadside, a small cube composes an elevated portal – an integrated carport and office tower. From there, a tangential path extending the entrance gangway beams over the declining meadow to the larger cube. The two-story dwelling is pushed way out to the area's northern margin, to the next edge and under the trees. Prefabricated parts of high-insulated, multi-layer wood and a combination of fixed and openable glazings form a climatic envelope. The dimly gleaming skin of broad shuttering panels gives the clear prisms a fine, furniture-like flair. In spite of minimized expenditures, the basic, transitory character of the entire property is set of to advantage with an ample extent of noblesse. The most simply shielded roof terrace is accessible over a roof hatch. The project was built in four weeks time. Adaptations to changed functionings and ways of life are no problem and are performed quickly.

The Noblesse of Transitoriness
Noblesse des Transitorischen

Demonstration der Vielseitigkeit des Holz-Box-Systems an einem Nordhang in einer Koppelung von Wohn- und Arbeitsbereichen. Das Grundstück wird durch die präzise und polare Setzung zweier modularer Baukörper in eine spannungsreiche Raumfigur umgeformt. Am südlichen Straßenrand bildet ein kleiner Kubus das aufgestelzte Portal – eine Integration von Carport und Büroturm. Ein tangentialer Weg in Verlängerung des Eingangsstegs strahlt von hier über die abfallende Wiese zu dem größeren Kubus hinüber. Das zweigeschoßige Wohnhaus ist ganz an den Nordrand des Grundes an die nächste Geländekante und unter die Bäume hinausgerückt. Hochgedämmte, mehrschichtige Holzfertigteile und eine Kombination aus fixen und öffenbaren Verglasungen bilden die Klimahülle. Die matt schimmernde Außenhaut aus großflächigen Schaltafeln gibt den klaren Prismen ein feines, möbelhaftes Flair. Der transitorische Grundcharakter des Ganzen kommt trotz minimierten Aufwands mit beachtlicher Noblesse zur Geltung. Über einen Dachausstieg ist die einfachst abgeschirmte Dachterrasse des Wohnhauses erreichbar. Die gesamte Bauzeit betrug vier Wochen. Eine Anpassung an veränderte Funktions- und Lebensweisen ist rasch und unproblematisch durchführbar.

View to the Job Box and gangway to the street
Blick zur Jobbox mit Steg zur Straße

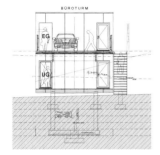

View from the street; ground floor, upper floor Dwelling Box
Blick von der Straße; Erdgeschoß, Obergeschoß Wohnbox

A Market to Stage the Location
Markt inszeniert den Ort

Unique among supermarkets, Mpreis does without a corporate identity attached to its more than 100 buildings in Tirol. Instead, the entire plant and the architecture is tailored for the respective location and various young local architects and international planners have been called upon. The construction in Kematen offers a column-free hall, 18 x 80 m, located along a traffic junction on the village's west end. Adjacent to many smaller buildings, the large volume is highly discrete in terms of proportions and materiality, set calmly on a meadow slightly inclined to the north. The south side, visible from a large distance and adorned with 'untouched' nature in the foreground, is largely closed and arranged with sizeable façade elements of prepatinated larchen sandwich panels. The hall's north side is fully paned and suggestively draws the panorama of the opposite Martinswand into the interior. The steel girders filled with concrete and the fixed glazings varying in size together constitute a relaxed lattice. The pale gray stone floor heats the entirety and is fed by geothermic energy gathered by collectors under the 1000 m² of parking space. Sections for collaborators and offices make up an inserted gallery on the south wall's inside; container-like storage facilities, set off by color, form a low counterpart for the gallery.

Für eine Supermarktkette einzigartig, verzichtet Mpreis auf eine Corporate Identity seiner bisher über 100 Bauten in Tirol. Stattdessen wird die gesamte Anlage und die Architektur jeweils für den Ort maßgeschneidert und werden dazu ganz verschiedene, jüngere Architekten aus der Region, aber auch internationale Planer herangezogen. Der Bau in Kematen bietet eine 18 x 80 m große, stützenfreie Halle, situiert an einem Straßenknoten am Westende des Ortes. Neben den viel kleineren Nachbarbauten ist das große Volumen in Proportion und Materialität sehr diskret und gelassen an die leicht nach Norden geneigte Wiese gelagert. Die Südseite, aus großer Distanz und mit ‚unberührter' Natur im Vordergrund sichtbar, ist weitgehend geschlossen, gegliedert mit großen Fassadenelementen aus vorpatinierten Dreischichtplatten in Lärche. Nach Norden ist die Halle vollflächig verglast und holt das Panorama der gegenüberliegenden Martinswand suggestiv in den Innenraum herein. Die ausbetonierten Stahlprofile bilden mit den größenmäßig variierenden Fixverglasungen ein optisch entspanntes Flechtwerk. Der hellgraue Steinboden heizt das Ganze, gespeist durch Erdwärme aus Kollektoren unter dem 1000 m² großen Parkplatz. Mitarbeiterbereiche und Büros bilden innen an der Südwand eine eingeschobene Galerie, containerartige Lagerbereiche, farbig abgesetzt, bilden dazu außerhalb ein niederes Pendant.

Ground plan; interior; north side; southern view
Grundriss; Innenraum; Nordseite; Südansicht

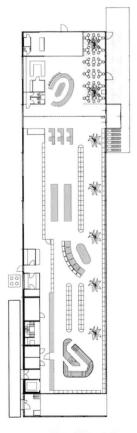

Beyond the Rustic and Romantic
Jenseits von Rustikal-Romantik

The shingle façade and roof form comply with the strict formalistic building regulations in Lech. Conversely, the interior of the simple volume offers a modern, urban-sportive alternative to the worthy rusticity shown by the neighboring lavish lodgings. Twelve apartments rented on a long-term basis are used chiefly by hotel employees, skiing instructors and other seasonal commercialists. Each of these small accommodations enjoys a loggia, a central sanitary and kitchen cell equipped with sleeping places that can be set up on both sides and shielded by sliding partitions. Extensive panings open the rooms to the access balcony and the loggias, blinds and shelves serve as variable screens. The surfaces given to the walls and the interior are limited to two materials: unprocessed fir and refined shuttering panels. Parking areas and surprisingly light-flooded side rooms for common use are located in the basement: a sauna, bathroom, resting rooms, cellar sections; a solar façade on the valley side. The project financed by the Kathans, albeit not immediately reconstructed by outsiders, is revolutionary for Arlberg tourist building and its rigid clichés, a pioneer achievement that should not be underestimated.

Schindelfassade und Dachform genügen der strengen, formalistischen Bausatzung von Lech. Das Innere des einfachen Volumens bietet dagegen eine moderne, urban-sportive Alternative zur biederen Rustikalität der benachbarten Nobelherbergen. Es sind zwölf langfristig vermietete Appartements, vor allem von Angestellten der Hotels, von Skilehrern und anderen saisonalen Dienstleistern genützt. Jede dieser Garçonnieren verfügt über eine Loggia, eine zentrale Sanitär- und Küchenzelle mit beidseitig situierbaren Schlafplätzen, die durch Schiebewände abgeschirmt werden können. Vollflächige Verglasungen öffnen die Räume zum Laubengang und zu den Loggien, Jalousien und Regale dienen als variabler Sichtschutz. Die Oberflächen von Wänden und Interieur sind auf zwei Materialien reduziert: unbehandeltes Tannenholz sowie beschichtete, edel verarbeitete Schaltafeln. Stellplätze und überraschend lichterfüllte, gemeinsam nutzbare Nebenräume liegen im Untergeschoß: Sauna, Bad, Ruheräume, Kellerabteile; Solarfassade an der Talseite. Für Außenstehende nicht gleich nachvollziehbar, doch für das in Klischees erstarrte touristische Bauen am Arlberg ist dieses von den Geschwistern Kathan finanzierte Projekt revolutionär, eine nicht zu unterschätzende Pionierleistung.

Ground plan; northwestern view; east side
Grundriss; NW-Ansicht; Ostseite

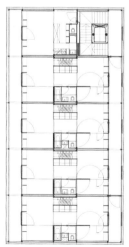

Adler Apartbox System, Hochkrumbach, Vorarlberg, 1998
Apartbox-System Adler

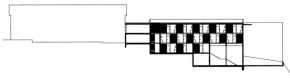

Extension of an old hotel at a height of 1600 m
Erweiterung eines alten Hotels in 1600 m Höhe

Holz Box Tirol
Colingasse 3, A–6020 Innsbruck
Tel +43-512-56 14 78, Fax +43-512-56 14 78-55
mailbox@holzbox.at, www.holzbox.at

Erich Strolz, born in 1959, grew up in Warth (Hochkrumbach), studied in Graz and Innsbruck, was awarded his diploma in 1989.
Armin Kathan, born in 1961, grew up in Lech, studied in Innsbruck and Vienna.
Joint office since 1993.
Buildings, projects (select): 1998–2001: Adler Apartbox System, Hochkrumbach, Vorarlberg (nominated in 2000 for the State's Prize for Economic Building / Tourism and Architecture); Rote Wand Apartbox System, Lech-Zug, Vorarlberg (1999 Vorarlberg Prize for Wooden Building); Kar Apartbox System, Lech, Vorarlberg (honorable mention, 2001 Vorarlberg Prize for Wooden Building); Mrs. Hitt Liftbox, Seegrube/ Innsbruck; Jagdgasse Row Houses, Innsbruck (1st BTV Clients Prize Tirol, 1999; honorable mention, 2001 Tirol Prize for Wooden Building); Hauser-Horntrich sfd, Natters, Tirol; Dwelling Box and Job Box, Klosterneuburg, Lower Austria (2001 Lower Austrian Prize for Wooden Building); Minibox, Innsbruck (honorable mention, 2001 Tirol Prize for Wooden Building); Mpreis Grocery Supermarket, Kematen; Altmann sfd, Innsbruck; Auduna Apartment House, Serfaus; Wanner Multi-Family Dwelling, Gerlos; all in Tirol; Crete Varibox Holiday House, Greece.
Planned: Wolkenstein Dwelling, Merano, South Tirol; Behmann Department Store, Egg, Vorarlberg; Stuhlfelden Grocery Supermarket, Salzburg.

Erich Strolz, geboren 1959, aufgewachsen in Warth (Hochkrumbach), Studium in Graz und Innsbruck, Diplom 1989.
Armin Kathan, geboren 1961, aufgewachsen in Lech, Studium in Innsbruck und Wien.
Seit 1993 gemeinsames Büro.
Bauten, Projekte (Auswahl): 1998–2001 Apartbox-System Adler, Hochkrumbach, Vorarlberg (Nominierung für den Staatspreis für Wirtschaftsbauten / Tourismus und Architektur 2000); Apartbox-System Rote Wand, Lech-Zug, Vorarlberg (Vorarlberger Holzbaupreis 1999); Apartbox-System Kar, Lech, Vorarlberg (Anerkennung Vorarlberger Holzbaupreis 2001); Liftbox Frau Hitt, Seegrube / Innsbruck; Reihenhausanlage Jagdgasse, Innsbruck (1. BTV-Bauherrenpreis Tirol 1999; Anerkennung Holzbaupreis Tirol 2001); EFH Hauser-Horntrich, Natters, Tirol; Wohnbox und Jobbox, Klosterneuburg, NÖ (NÖ Holzbaupreis 2001); Minibox, Innsbruck (Anerkennung Holzbaupreis Tirol 2001); Lebensmittelsupermarkt Mpreis, Kematen; EFH Altmann, Innsbruck; Apartmenthaus Auduna, Serfaus; Mehrfamilienhaus Wanner, Gerlos; alle Tirol; Varibox-Ferienhaus Kreta, Griechenland. In Planung: Wohnhaus Wolkenstein, Meran, Südtirol; Kaufhaus Behmann, Egg, Vorarlberg; Lebensmittelmarkt Stuhlfelden, Salzburg.

Dwelling Box Row Houses / Reihenhausanlage Wohnbox, Sistrans
Client / Bauherr: Jenewein Wohnbau
Statics / Statik: Ingo Gehrer

Mpreis Grocery Supermarket / Lebensmittelsupermarkt Mpreis, Kematen
Client / Bauherr: Mpreis WarenvertriebsGmbH
Statics / Statik: Alfred Brunnsteiner

Minibox
Client / Bauherr: Holz Box Tirol

Jagdgasse Row Houses / Reihenhausanlage Jagdgasse, Innsbruck
Client / Bauherr: Familie Zanon-Danler-Hüttemann
Statics / Statik: Ingo Gehrer

Dwelling Box and Job Box / Wohnbox und Jobbox, Klosterneuburg
Client / Bauherr: Familie Basura-Seelos
Statics / Statik: Ingo Gehrer

Kar Apartbox System / Apartbox-System Kar, Lech
Client / Bauherr: Geschwister Kathan
Statics / Statik: Hans Fuchs and / und Ingo Gehrer

Adler Apartbox System / Apartbox-System Adler, Hochkrumbach
Client / Bauherr: Markus Strolz
Statics / Statik: Ingo Gehrer

Holz Box Team and single-project collaborators / Holz Box-Team und MitarbeiterInnen bei
einzelnen Projekten: Erich Strolz, Armin Kathan, Bernhard Geiger, Ferdinand Reiter, Klaus
Vonier, Peter Wurmböck, Stefan Taschler, Christian Haag, Manuel Breu, Gerhard Reiter, Martin
Grafenauer, Christian Albrecht, Christoph Juen, Christian Klein, Verena Bohnert, Christof
Hrdlovics, Judith Simoni, Gerfried Schneider u. a.

Architekturzentrum Wien; Springer-Verlag Wien New York; Text: © Otto Kapfinger
Photo credits: © by the architects and: Gerda Eichholzer: 63, 67, 69; Bruno Klomfar: 75–77, 81; Günter
Kresser: 82; Günter Wett: 61, 65, 71–73, 79

one room   huber / meinhart

vision: perfect imperfection
vision: perfekte unvollkommenheit

their entry on the scene took a course contrary to the habitual. georg huber and karl meinhart approached their team identity not via trendy shop designs or trim single-family dwellings. actionist interventions and interdisciplinary analyses in salzburg city gave them their initial tread. their first collaborative competition dealt with structural measures to modernize a gigantic area in thessaloniki. at that time, the second-largest seaport in greece sought impulses for its role as 1997 european capital of culture. one room was awarded one of the main prizes in a procedure that involved experts and young teams from all over europe in multistage workshops. at the same time, meinhart attended to the 'public space' project together with salzburg cultural associations and the local 'initiative architektur'; and huber and meinhart accompanied a permanent study initiated by the eth zurich, developing urbanistic concepts for salzburg and giving rise, at the local level, to a fresh network with the relevant european discourse. in all these enterprises, their perspective was sharpened for the relative quality of a common architectural discussion that is attached merely to objects or isolated building projects. articulating the issues of location quality, the potential for follow-up use, the social and economic fields of activity in long-term urbanistic connections at the most up-to-date level – that is what subsequently formed the foundation for concrete building projects.

ihr auftritt in der szene verlief konträr zum gewohnten. georg huber und karl meinhart fanden nicht über trendige ladendesigns oder schmucke einfamilienhäuser zur teamidentität. ihre profilierung begann mit aktionistischen eingriffen und interdisziplinären analysen im salzburger stadtraum. ihr erster gemeinsamer wettbewerb be- handelte strukturmaßnahmen zur modernisierung eines riesigen areals in thessaloniki. die zweitgrößte hafenstadt griechenlands suchte damals impulse für die rolle als europas kulturhauptstadt 1997. in dem verfahren, das mit experten und jungen teams aus ganz europa in mehrstufigen workshops abgewickelt und an ort und stelle vertieft wurde, erhielt one room einen der hauptpreise. im selben zeitraum betreute meinhart mit salzburger kulturvereinen und der lokalen architektur-initiative die aktion ‚public space‘, begleiteten huber und meinhart eine ganzjährige studie der eth zürich, die städtebauliche konzepte für salzburg entwickelte und die auf lokaler ebene eine frische vernetzung mit dem einschlägigen europäischen diskurs bewirkte. in all diesen unternehmungen schärfte sich ihre sicht für die relativität der üblichen, bloß auf objekte oder isolierte bauprojekte fixierten architekturdiskussion. fragen der standortqualität, des nachnutzungs-potenzials, der sozialen und wirtschaftlichen wirkungsfelder in längerfristigen urbanistischen zusammenhängen auf dem aktuellsten

leopoldskron kindergarten, salzburg, hall
kindergarten leopoldskron, halle

in 1998, they were then awarded first prize at an invited architects' competition for the psv sports building. their kindergarten in leopoldskron won the european innovation competition in 1999. one year thereafter, they were awarded first prize in the invited salzburg/welserstraße housing competition and finally were successful, in 2001, in an EU single-tender action for an extension of the salzburg business school. the common denominator between the above and other designs is a quality that today belongs to many teams' rhetorical repertoire, yet is rarely conclusively materialized in building. this quality pertains to criteria converted in individual objects, gathered from analyzing a larger ambient in time and space: an aversion to architecture's isolated perfectionism for the benefit of preserving an openness in building for developments that exceed the superficiality of esthetic or punctually functionalist decision-making. 'landscape' is the term the scene discourse today gives to such sensitiveness. for one room, it is wide-awake, critical action against a fashion in urbanism reduced to object management – and in favor of the paradox, further-reaching perspective on buildings: acting as building stones of a 'city of perfect imperfection' yet to come.

niveau zu thematisieren – das bildete in der folge die grundlage für konkrete bauprojekte. 1998 folgte der 1. preis beim geladenen architektenwettbewerb für das psv-sportgebäude, 1999 der sieg im europaweiten innovationswettbewerb für den kindergarten leopoldskron, 2000 der 1. platz im geladenen wohnbauwettbewerb salzburg/welserstraße und 2001 der erfolg im EU-verhandlungsverfahren für die erweiterung der handelsakademie salzburg. gemeinsamer nenner dieser genannten und anderer entwürfe ist eine qualität, die heute zum rhetorischen repertoire vieler teams gehört, die aber nur selten eine schlüssige verwirklichung im gebauten findet. es ist die umsetzung von kriterien im einzelobjekt, die aus der analyse des größeren, raum-zeitlichen umfelds gewonnen wurden: eine abkehr vom isolierten perfektionismus der architektur zugunsten der erhaltung einer offenheit des gebauten für entwicklungen jenseits der vordergründig ästhetischen oder punktuell funktionalistischen entscheidung. im szene-diskurs läuft solche sensibilität heute unter dem weiten begriff ‚landschaft'. für one room ist es das hellwache, kritische agieren gegen die mode des auf objektmanagement reduzierten städtebaus – und für die paradoxe, weitergreifende sicht von gebäuden: als bausteine einer künftigen ‚stadt von perfekter unvollkommenheit'.

salzburg psv sports center, construction
psv-sportzentrum, rohbau

a crease in the meadow
knick in der wiese

this plot is located in a listed landscape, the rambling leopoldskron marshland. the kindergarten is equipped with a forecourt and an existing clubhouse and forms the public neighborhood spot. the topic was how a building could define its public role and mark the fringe of the landscape at the same time. huber / meinhart identified the particular issue and produced a convincing answer in a european union innovation competition. they formulated the location and its specific function by way of one single, simple measure – the meadowland was folded up on the plot's southeastern corner. the lawn vaults to become a rooftop, generates and covers a volume of space, at once to stay what it was – a ground and a meadow. a playing hill becoming a roof, a roof turning into a stage, linking up to the lower playground, the square and into the moorland. a paned incision along the northwestern side serves as an entrance and illuminates a two-story hall. the latter accesses the group rooms oriented to the south and east. topped by wooden elements, insulating courses and a green roof, a steel construction set upon a concrete slab with 9 m-deep foundation piles also feeds the heating and cooling system with geothermic energy. the roof profile forms low spandrels at the hallways' and rooms' ends, which are put to use as intimate, informal niches.

der baugrund liegt im landschaftsschutzgebiet, dem weitläufigen leopoldskroner moor. der kindergarten mit dem vorplatz und dem schon länger bestehenden vereinsheim bildet den öffentlichen ort der nachbarschaft. das thema war: wie definiert hier ein bau seine öffentliche rolle und markiert zugleich den rand der landschaft. huber/meinhart erkannten die spezielle frage und gaben in dem EU-weiten innovationsverfahren eine überzeugende antwort. sie formulierten den ort und seine spezifische funktion durch eine einzige, einfache maßnahme – das hochfalten des wiesengeländes an der südostecke des grundstücks. das rasenfeld wölbt sich auf, wird dachfläche, erzeugt und überdeckt ein raumvolumen, bleibt zugleich, was es war – wiese und gelände. spielhügel wird dach, dach wird spielfläche, die zum unteren spielfeld, zum vor-platz und in die moorlandschaft überleitet. ein verglaster einschnitt an der nordwestseite wirkt als eingang und belichtet eine zweigeschoßige halle. diese erschließt die nach süden und osten orientierten gruppen-räume. auf der betonplatte mit 9 m tiefen gründungspfählen, die auch erdwärme für das heiz- und kühlsystem liefern, steht eine stahlkon-struktion, gedeckt mit holzelementen, dämmschichten und dem grün-dach. die dachkontur bildet niedrige zwickel an den gang- und raumenden, die als intime, informelle nischen genützt werden.

conceptional model; view from the marshland
konzeptionelles modell; ansicht vom moor

one room huber / meinhart

ground plan first floor; section; views
grundriss erdgeschoß; schnitt; ansichten

entrance hall upper floor; hall with gallery
flurbereich obergeschoß; halle mit galerie

business school 1+2, conversion and extension, salzburg-lehen, planned
handelsakademie 1+2, umbau und erweiterung, in planung

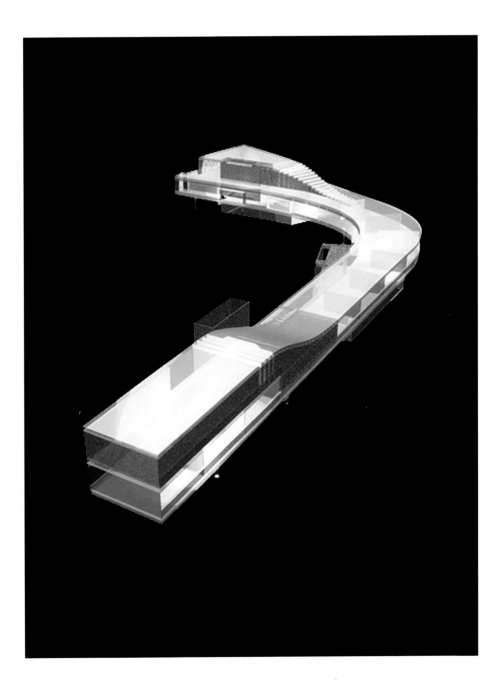

vision

where does architecture start?
wo beginnt architektur?

a large complex was to be extended for some 1000 students and separate evening classes for working people. opposed to the adjacent densification caused by a superstructure over old wings or the court, huber / meinhart were the only contestants to react with an approach to social and urban spaces. the existing structure's most prominent quality, its large court, was not affected, not even by the deep long-standing bodies equipped with many domelights. instead, its 'arbitrary' flow into the street space and the banks of the salzach was recognized as a weak point and corrected with the new building. comments roman höllbacher, 'they planted the new building in front of the old structure like a shield and thus lent it its very first real entrance hall and a face. the present court is even improved by the second developing in the new building's bracket. this subtle elaboration of quality, bringing together the previously open flanks, shows that architecture sets in long before detailed questions are asked, and that it may contribute to substantial decision-making in society only by way of such substantial ascertainments.' furthermore, while operations are fully maintained, disturbance is reduced to a minimum.

perfe

eine große anlage für rund 1000 schülerInnen mit gesondertem abendbetrieb für erwerbstätige muss erweitert werden. entgegen der naheliegenden verdichtung durch überbauung von alttrakten oder des hofes reagierten huber / meinhart im rahmen der konkurrenz als einzige mit einem sozial- und stadträumlichen ansatz. die beste qualität des bestandes, der große hof, wird nicht angetastet, auch nicht die mit vielen lichtkuppeln ausgerüsteten, tiefen bestandsbauten. statt dessen wird die schwachstelle des altbaus, sein ‚beliebiges' ausrinnen zum straßenraum und zum salzachufer hin erkannt und mit dem neubau korrigiert. dazu roman höllbacher: ‚gleich einem schild pflanzen sie den neubau vor den bestand und verschaffen ihm damit erstmals ein wirkliches entree und ein gesicht. der bestehende hof wird durch den in der spange des neubaus entstehenden zweiten hof sogar noch verbessert. dieses subtile herausarbeiten der qualität, indem die bislang offenen flanken zusammengeführt werden, zeigt, dass architektur lange vor detailfragen ansetzt und dass sie nur über diese inhaltlichen bestimmungen an den wesentlichen gesellschaftlichen entscheidungen partizipiert.' überdies entstehen so durch die bauführung bei voller aufrechterhaltung des betriebs die geringsten störungen.

cad renderings, curved bracket along the old building; plans
gekurvte spange am altbau; grundrisse

unvollkommenheit

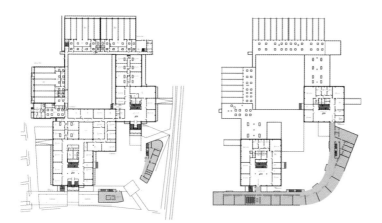

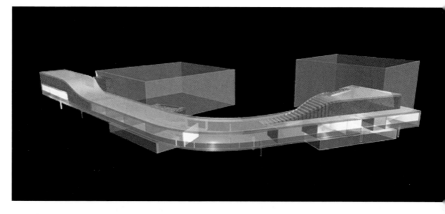

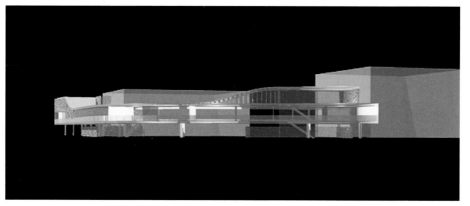

sports linking the disparate
sport verknüpft disparates

alongside the existing playing fields, a clubhouse was to be designed for the largest local association – a hall 30 by 16 m, to accommodate judo, taekwondo and other sports, in addition to wardrobes and sanitary facilities. the place is particular in that it forms an interface between the commercial strip in the south of town (with large container buildings) and the ample, protected park area stretching between freisaal and hellbrunn castles. on the northern side of the fields, a heavily frequented avenue links the 'alpenstraße' automobile and shopping zone with the quiet green space. the project selected in an invited competition concentrates the cubage of residential occupancies at the plot's northern end and gives the impression of a gateway, with its trees and tall neighboring buildings, right across where the avenue opens. the main volume being pillared, the location is given a strong accent and a dialog is opened with the considerable volumes around. on the other hand, the open ground floor emphasizes the transparency, ease and continuity arising from the flow of movement into the green. the 'free' form signalizes both the sporting utilization and a link with nature. anchored to a concrete core, the steel skeleton is shelved with concrete floors and wood-glass elements, altogether enveloped by a silvery, holohedral sheet skin.

für den größten lokalen verein war neben bestehenden freiplätzen ein klubhaus zu entwerfen, zusätzlich zu garderoben und sanitärräumen eine 30 x 16 m große halle für judo und taekwondo, aber auch für andere sportarten. der platz war insofern besonders, als er eine schnittstelle bildet zwischen dem commercial strip im süden der stadt (mit großen containerbauten) und dem weiträumigen, geschützten grüngebiet zwischen den schlössern freisaal und hellbrunn. an der nordseite der plätze verbindet eine stark frequentierte allee die auto- und einkaufswelt der alpenstraße mit dem ruhigen grünraum. das im geladenen wettbewerb ausgewählte projekt konzentriert die baumasse am nordende des grundstücks und schafft im gegenüber mit den bäumen und den hohen nachbarbauten eine torwirkung am beginn der allee. durch das aufständern des hauptvolumens wird die situation einerseits kräftig akzentuiert und ein dialog mit den beachtlichen volumina der umgebung erreicht, andererseits betont das offen gehaltene erdgeschoß die transparenz, die leichtigkeit und kontinuität des bewegungsflusses zum grünraum. die ‚freie' form signalisiert die sportive nutzung und die nahtstelle zur natur. das stahlgerippe ankert am betonkern, ist mit betondecken und holz-glaselementen ausgefacht und hat eine silbrige, vollflächig aufgebrachte folienhaut.

sections; view of the carcass
schnitte; ansicht rohbau

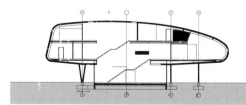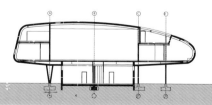

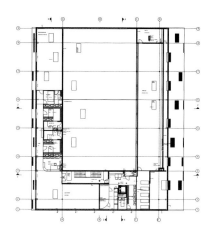

construction; building phases; model; ground plan third floor
konstruktion; bauphasen; modell; grundriss 2. stock

urban space, a spatial contract
stadtraum als raumvertrag

from throughout the eu, 220 teams sketched plans to develop the areas called the 'west arc' in the hinterland of the city center. interspersed with large fallow fields, abandoned tobacco storehouses, fragments of residential districts and old barrack wings, this periphery is located some two kilometers away from the coast and represents a domain of both hope and speculation for the rapidly growing metropolis. macedonia and bulgaria are barely 100 km away, and turkey just 250 km. one room and four other prizewinners were invited to attend workshops, to deepen and coordinate their approaches with local and international experts. said edouard bru, 'the meinhart / huber project develops a special type of space for each location. the tobacco warehouses are remodelled for new uses as public space with their interior being extrapolated outwards in the form of a carpet. this arrangement extends to the newly constructed buildings. with its small number of appropriate ambitions and a degree of minimalism in the form and media, this project really does supply the public authorities with a strategy for the creation of true urbanism.' apart from ideas to interlace the urban fragments, the plan called for 'allotment contracts' to be settled with the city: a local integration of public expanses in terms of both old and new stuctures, holding rights and obligations of usufruct for the individual building contractors and institutions.

220 teams aus den eu-ländern erarbeiteten pläne zur entwicklung der ‚west-arc‘ genannten areale im hinterland des stadtkerns. diese mit großen brachflächen, aufgelassenen tabakspeichern, fragmenten von wohnvierteln und alten kasernentrakten durchsetzte peripherie liegt gut zwei kilometer hinter der küste und bietet ein hoffnungs-, aber auch ein spekulationsfeld für die rasch wachsende millionenstadt. mazedonien und bulgarien sind kaum 100 km, die türkei nur 250 km entfernt. one room und vier weitere preisträger wurden zu workshops geladen, vertieften und koordinierten ihre ansätze mit lokalen und internationalen experten. edouard bru: ‚the meinhart / huber project develops a special type of space for each location. the tobacco warehouses are remodelled for new uses as public space with their interior being extrapolated outwards in the form of a carpet. this arrangement extends to the newly constructed buildings. with its small number of appropriate ambitions and a degree of minimalism in the form and media, this project really does supply the public authorities with a strategy for the creation of true urbanism.' neben ideen zur vernetzung der stadtfragmente propagierte der plan ‚parzellenverträge‘ mit der stadt: die lokale integration öffentlicher flächen zu alt- und neubauten mit nutzungsrechten und -pflichten für die einzelnen bauträger und institutionen.

extension of storehouses, integration of public areas
erweiterung der lagerhäuser, integration öffentlicher flächen

the west arc for thessaloniki, international urbanistic competition
internationaler städtebaulicher wettbewerb

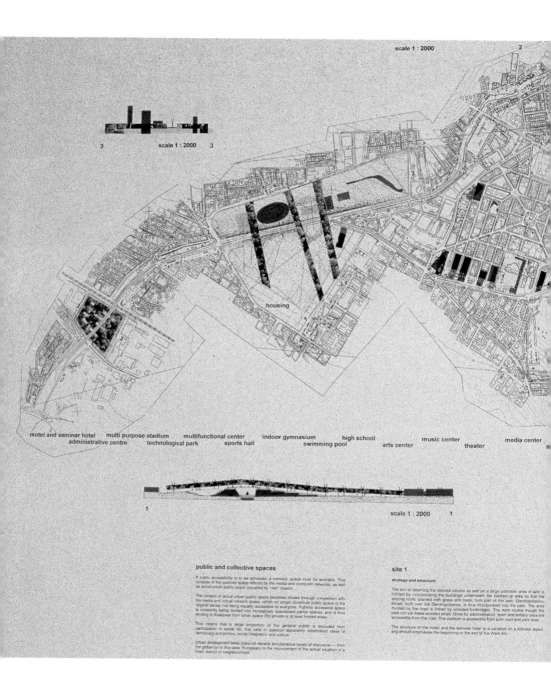

scale 1 : 2000

3   scale 1 : 2000   3

housing

motel and seminar hotel   multi purpose stadium   multifunctional center   indoor gymnasium   high school   music center   media center
administrative centre   technological park   sports hall   swimming pool   arts center   theater

1   scale 1 : 2000   1

public and collective spaces

If public accessibility is to be achieved, a common space must be available. This consists of the publicity space offered by the media and computer networks, as well as actual urban public space occupied by "real" objects.

The content of actual urban public space becomes diluted through competition with the media and virtual network space, which no longer constitute public space in the original sense, not being equally accessible to everyone. Publicly accessible space is constantly being divided into increasingly specialised partial spaces, and is thus tending to disappear from urban space into private or at least limited areas.

This means that a large proportion of the general public is excluded from participation in social life; this calls in question apparently established ideas of democracy and politics, social integration and culture.

Urban development takes place on several simultaneous levels of discussion — from the global (or in this case European) to the improvement of the actual situation in a town, district or neighbourhood.

site 1

strategy and structure:

The aim of retaining the desired volume as well as a large unbroken area of land is fulfilled by incorporating the buildings underneath the banked-up area so that the sloping roofs, planted with grass and trees, form part of the park. Dendropotamou Street, built over the Dendropotamos, is thus incorporated into the park. The area divided by the road is linked by wooded footbridges. The main routes through the park run via three wooded strips. Units for administration, sport and tertiary uses are accessible from the road. The stadium is accessible from both road and park level.

The structure of the motel and the seminar hotel is a variation on a fortress layout and should emphasise the beginning or the end of the West Arc.

one room   huber / meinhart

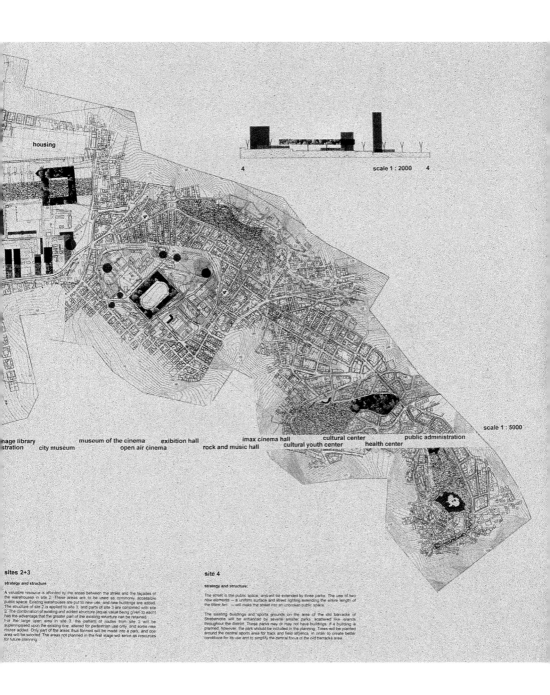

housing

4   scale 1 : 2000   4

scale 1 : 5000

nage library   museum of the cinema   exibition hall   imax cinema hall   cultural center   public administration
stration   city museum   open air cinema   rock and music hall   cultural youth center   health center

sites 2+3

strategy and structure

A valuable resource is afforded by the areas between the street and the façades of
the warehouses in site 2. These areas are to be used as commonly accessible
public space. Existing warehouses are put to new use, and new buildings are added.
The structure of site 2 is applied to site 3, and parts of site 3 are combined with site
2. The combination of existing and added structure (equal value being given to each)
has the advantage that the greater part of the existing structure can be retained.
For the large open area in site 3, the pattern of routes from site 2 will be
superimposed upon the existing one, altered for pedestrian use only, and some new
routes added. Only part of the areas thus formed will be made into a park, and one
area will be wooded. The areas not planned in the first stage will serve as resources
for future planning.

site 4

strategy and structure:

The street is the public space, and will be extended by three parks. The use of two
new elements — a uniform surface and street lighting extending the entire length of
the West Arc — will make the street into an unbroken public space.

The existing buildings and sports grounds on the area of the old barracks of
Strebersdorf will be enhanced by several smaller parks scattered like islands
throughout the district. These parks may or may not have buildings. If a building is
planned, however, the park should be included in the planning. Trees will be planted
around the central sports area for track and field athletics, in order to create better
conditions for its use and to simplify the central focus of the old barracks area.

105

antifascist memorial, arts competition with heimo zobernig, 1st prize 2001–02, salzburg, 2002
antifaschismus mahnmal, kunstwettbewerb mit heimo zobernig, 1. preis

cad perspective, view from the main railroad station
cad-perspektive, blick vom hauptbahnhof

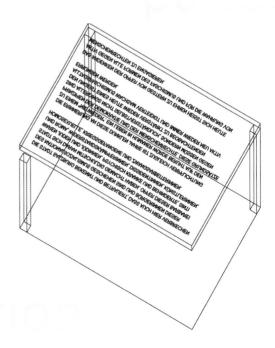

one room huber/meinhart
hellbrunnerstraße 3/5, a–5020 salzburg
tel/fax +43-662-84 17 12, +43-662-84 23 64
oneroom@aon.at, www.oneroom.at

georg huber, born in hallein, salzburg, in 1960. studied architecture in graz, awarded diploma in 1990. own office in salzburg since 1996. chaired the initiative architektur salzburg from 1996 to 98. member of the salzburg advisory board for architecture from 1998 to 2001.
karl meinhart, born in vöcklabruck, upper austria, in 1954. studied architecture at the tu in vienna, awarded diploma in 1986. own office in vienna since 1993 and in salzburg since 1996. board member of the initiative architektur salzburg from 1996 to 2001. lecturer at the salzburg mozarteum in 2002.
joint studio and working group since 1997.
buildings and projects (select): the west arc for thessaloniki for the european cultural capital, 1997–2000; salzburg taxham, study project elaborated with the eth zurich, department of city planning, 1997; police athletic club sports center, experts selection procedure, salzburg, 1998-2002; icon – urban images, exhibition project, galerie fotohof, salzburg, 1998; leopoldskron kindergarten, salzburg, 1999–2001 (2002 salzburg energy prize); gymnasium redevelopment bg2, salzburg-lehen, 2000. under construction: salzburg-maxglan housing development. planned: business school 1+2, conversion and extension, eu single-tender action, 1ˢᵗ prize, salzburg-lehen.

georg huber, geboren 1960 in hallein, salzburg. architekturstudium in graz, diplom 1990. eigenes büro seit 1996 in salzburg. 1996–98 vorsitzender der initiative architektur salzburg. 1998–2001 mitglied des fachbeirates architektur des landes salzburg.
karl meinhart, geboren 1954 in vöcklabruck, OÖ. architekturstudium an der tu wien, diplom 1986. eigenes büro seit 1993 in wien und seit 1996 in salzburg. 1996–2001 vorstandsmitglied der initiative architektur salzburg. 2002 lehrtätigkeit im mozarteum salzburg. atelier- und arbeitsgemeinschaft seit 1997.
bauten und projekte (auswahl): 1997–2000 the west arc for thessaloniki, europäische kulturhauptstadt; 1997 salzburg taxham, studienprojekt mit der eth zürich, institut für städtebau; 1998–2002 polizeisportverein sportzentrum, salzburg; 1998 icon – urban images, ausstellungsprojekt, galerie fotohof, salzburg; 1999–2001 kindergarten leopoldskron, salzburg (salzburger landesenergiepreis 2002); 2000 turnhallen-sanierung bg2, salzburg-lehen. in bau: wohnbebauung salzburg-maxglan. in planung: handelsakademie 1+2, umbau und erweiterung, eu-weites verhandlungsverfahren, salzburg-lehen.

leopoldskron kindergarten, european innovation competition, 2-stage, 1st prize / kindergarten
leopoldskron, salzburg, europaweiter innovationswettbewerb, 2-stufig, 1. preis
client / bauherr: salzburg city, architectural engineering office / stadt salzburg, hochbauamt,
ssw bauträger
collaborators / mitarbeiterinnen: brigitte huber-theissl, barbara linsberger, martina schaberl
statics / statik: rds eugen schuler, dornbirn
concept for engineering of services and power / energie-, haustechnikkonzept: tb michael
gutbrunner, dornbirn
constructional physics / bauphysik: a.b.o. rosenheim, georg stahl, udo bergfeld
building artwork / kunst am bau: christine and / und irene hohenbüchler with / mit werner
feiersinger, eichgraben
photos / fotos: margherita spiluttini

salzburg police athletic club sports center, experts selection procedure, 1st prize /
polizeisportverein sportzentrum salzburg, gutachterverfahren, 1. preis
project partner / projektpartner: walter schuster
client / bauherr: police athletic club / psv objektvermietung II
collaborator / mitarbeiterin: martina schaberl
statics / statik: rds eugen schuler, dornbirn / kurt haargassner, salzburg
supervision / projektmanagement: sabfinanz

business school 1+2, conversion and extension, eu single-tender action, 1st prize /
handelsakademie 1+2, umbau und erweiterung, eu-weites verhandlungsverfahren, 1. preis,
salzburg-lehen
client / bauherr: bundesimmobiliengesellschaft big / imb
collaborators / mitarbeiter: katrin grimm, martina schaberl, walter schuster

the west arc for thessaloniki, international urbanistic competition, 1st prize / saloniki,
internationaler städtebaulicher wettbewerb, 1. preis
client / bauherr: european cultural capital, ministry of the environment, planning and public
works, europan / europäische kulturhauptstadt thessaloniki
publication / publikation: the west arc for thessaloniki, new collective spaces in the
contemporary city, edited by yorgos simeoforidis, west arc competition europan for cultural
capital of europe thessaloniki (2000)

antifascist memorial, international 2-stage arts competition with heimo zobernig, 1st prize /
antifaschismus mahnmal, internationaler 2-stufiger kunstwettbewerb mit heimo zobernig,
1. preis, südtiroler platz, salzburg
collaborator / mitarbeiterin: barbara linsberger
statics / statik: rds eugen schuler, dornbirn

with the kind support of / mit freundlicher unterstützung von:
AREA handelsgesellschaft m.b.h, bayerhamerstraße 5, a–5020 salzburg
spiluttinibaugmbh, dr. franz hain-straße 8, a–5620 schwarzach im pongau

AREA

SPILUTTINI

pool

Ramp Becomes Room
Raumwerdung der Rampe

Their contribution to Vienna's architectural accomplishments of the 1990s is epochal, for the 'Sargfabrik' housing developed together with Johann Winter marks a typological and urbanistic milestone in that decade's mass of local residential building. After BKK 2 broke up, the members forming 'pool' in 1998 intensified the principles that were noticeable in the inclined planes of the Sargfabrik or the Linz dormitory to a new significance and along a whole scale of measures. Simply spoken, pool architecture unfolds in the ramp's spatial genesis. The inclined plane emancipates itself from a mere communication band to a catalyst for the structure's entire form. From the smallest row house to the most comprehensive projects in urban planning, inclined planes of movement create a dynamically flowing, interlocking system that encompasses spatial parts and levels of usage. By grafting further occupancies – by making the ramp 'habitable' – the unidimensional theme is given ambivalence and crucial energy: no formal whim, but rather a creative reassessment of pertinent economic constraints into creative value added. Le Corbusier had made a start with a 'ramp in the house', and Loos had demanded that stairs should 'vanish' from the vertically opened constructional organism; imperceptible steps and plateaus that adhere to space were to link shifting and superimposing levels. But the automobile, the primary cause of ramps, still failed to

Ihr Beitrag zum Wiener Architekturgeschehen der 1990er Jahre ist epochal, denn die gemeinsam mit Johann Winter realisierte Wohnanlage ‚Sargfabrik' markiert typologisch und urbanistisch einen Meilenstein in der Masse der lokalen Wohnbauleistungen dieses Jahrzehnts. Nach der Auflösung von BKK 2 steigerten die 1998 als ‚pool' Neuformierten die in der Sargfabrik oder beim Linzer Studentenheim in den schrägen Hauptebenen schon spürbaren Prinzipien auf der ganzen Skala der Maßstäbe zu neuer Signifikanz. Vereinfacht könnte man sagen: die Architektur von pool entfaltet sich in der Raumwerdung der Rampen. Die schiefe Ebene emanzipiert sich vom bloßen Verkehrsband zum Katalysator der ganzen Baugestalt. Vom kleinsten Reihenhaus bis zu großen Städtebauprojekten erzeugen schräge Bewegungsflächen den dynamisch fließenden Verbund aller Raumpartien und Nutzebenen. Durch die Aufpfropfung weiterer Nutzungen – durch die ‚Bewohnbarmachung' der Rampe – wird aus dem eindimensionalen Thema ein ambivalentes und hochenergetisches: keine formale Marotte, sondern kreative Umwertung ökonomischer, sachlicher Zwänge zum gestalterischen Mehrwert. Le Corbusier hatte mit der ‚Rampe im Haus' begonnen, und Loos hatte gefordert, die Stiege im vertikal geöffneten Bauorganismus solle ‚verschwinden'; Niveauwechsel und -überlagerungen sollten durch unmerkliche, zum Raum gehörige Stufen und Plateaus

House in spe, Vienna
Haus in spe

form an integral moment for constructional genesis. Garage planning was to become a specialist segment, and the 'car-friendly city' a functionalist nightmare. pool made a virtue of such necessity. The departure ramp down to a minimal house's roofed parking space, for instance, refuses to be a secondary episode, an appendage shy of architecture, but instead represents a creative nucleus for the entire building. Transposed to larger dimensions, that is to say: to penetrate into the 'underworld' of houses, the traffic-sensitive permeation of quarters, gives the whole disposition a new sense of continuity. Of course, the New York Five and others already took up the ramp in the seventies and eighties, and Koolhaas rediscovered the spiral as a constructional principle or the brisance of spatial wedges. Yet I am unaware of any comparably 'dense package' of ramp arguments as pool's 'House in spe'. No speculative architecture sculpture, but optimized useable areas and spatial experiences in the smallest dimensions, the classical Viennese Raumplan accelerated to the car-bound housing of our times; spatial complexity enchased with strong colors as a primary, robust achievement to which statics and technology, detailed language and homogeneous materialization are subordinated.

verbunden werden. Immer noch aber war das Auto, der primäre Erreger von Rampen, kein integrales Moment der baulichen Genese. Garagenplanung wurde zum Spezialistensegment, die ‚autogerechte Stadt' ein funktionalistischer Alptraum. Aus solcher Not macht pool eine Tugend. Die Abfahrtsrampe zum gedeckten Stellplatz eines Minimalhauses etwa bleibt nicht sekundäre Episode, architekturscheues Anhängsel, sie wird vielmehr zum gestalterischen Nukleus des ganzen Gebäudes. Umgemünzt auf größere Dimensionen heißt das: aus dem Eindringen in die ‚Unterwelt' von Häusern, aus der verkehrlichen Durchdringung von Quartieren wird eine neue Kontinuität der gesamten Disposition. Natürlich haben New York Five und andere die Rampe schon in den siebziger und achtziger Jahren wieder aufgegriffen, hat Koolhaas die Spirale als Bauprinzip und die Brisanz von Raumkeilen wiederentdeckt. Eine vergleichbar ‚dichte Packung' von Rampen-Argumenten, wie das ‚Haus in spe' von pool ist mir nicht bekannt: keine spekulative Architektur-Skulptur, sondern Optimierung von Nutzflächen und Raumerlebnissen auf kleinster Fläche, Beschleunigung des klassischen Wiener Raumplans in das autogebundene Hausen unserer Zeit; mit starken Farben gefasste Raumkomplexität als primäre, robuste Leistung, der sich Statik und Technologie, Detailsprache und homogene Materialisierung lakonisch unterordnen.

Urbanistic concept, KDAG Grounds, Vienna, 1998; detail
Städtebauliches Konzept, KDAG-Gründe; Ausschnitt

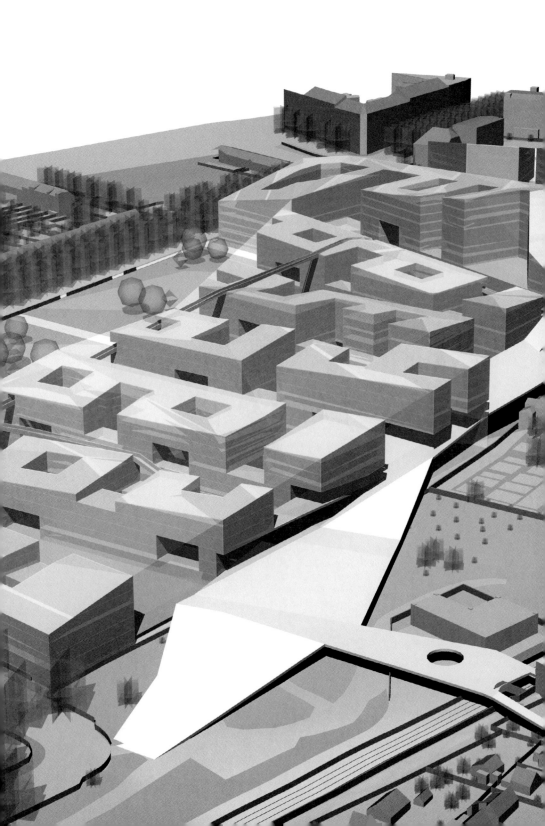

Locksmith's Hall and Bar
Schlosserei mit Bar

The last building in a series of industrial plants on the outskirts was constructed in front of a flat landscape, a monolithic block in the fields. The free-stretched steel frame structure is lined with Heraklith insulating material on the inside and paneled with corroding steel plates on the outside. The glazings given to the quadratic openings are flush with the steel façade, the floor is of smoothed concrete. All's what it is. The particular note derives from the specific 'pool' tendency to translate a given building's driveway and entrance into a spatial theme and to graft additional functions to commonly monocausal accesses. Here, the front part of the hall contains a slightly sunk storage. The incision made for the departure and switching ramps is roofed by an inclined steel plate and a pedestrian ramp. The latter are extended into the interior in terms of a further vaulted 'landscape' of inclines, steps and ramps that roof the stock room, open to the hall, and that serve as a location for stopovers and sociability. Equipped with a counter and sanitary facilities, the walk-in, circumventable mound of steel plates with large glass walls giving to the hall and street not only satisfies the laborer's needs. At night, it changes into a public bar. The slanting counter has become a venue for all of Trumau and surroundings.

Als letzter einer Reihe von Industrieanlagen am Ortsrand steht der Bau frei vor der ebenen Landschaft, ein monolithischer Block auf dem Feld. Die frei gespannte Stahlrahmenkonstruktion ist innen mit Heraklith gedämmt, außen mit rostenden Stahlplatten verkleidet. Die quadratischen Öffnungen sind bündig mit der Stahlfassade verglast, der Boden ist geglätteter Beton. Alles ist, wie es ist. Die besondere Note kommt aus der spezifischen pool-Tendenz, Zufahrt und Eingang des Bauwerks in ein räumliches Thema umzusetzen und der üblicherweise monokausalen Erschließung zusätzliche Funktionen aufzupfropfen. Hier enthält der vordere Teil der Halle ein etwas abgesenktes Lager. Der Geländeeinschnitt der Abfahrts- und Rangierrampe wird von einer schrägen Stahlplatte und einer Fußgängerrampe überdacht. Diese beiden setzen sich im Innenraum in eine weiter aufgewölbte ‚Landschaft' von Schrägen, Stufen und Rampen fort, welche den zur Halle offenen Lagerraum überdachen und als Sozial- und Aufenthaltsbereich der Belegschaft dienen. Ausgestattet mit einem Tresen und Sanitärräumen dient der begeh- und umgehbare Hügel aus Stahlplatten mit den großen Glaswänden zur Halle und zur Straße nicht nur den Bedürfnissen der Arbeiter. Nachts verwandelt er sich in eine öffentliche Bar. Der schräge Tresen wurde inzwischen ein Treffpunkt für ganz Trumau und Umgebung.

Box, slope and slanting bar: metal on the meadow
Box, Böschung und schräge Bar: Metall auf der Wiese

pool

trum, Locksmith's Hall and Bar
Schlosserhalle mit Bar

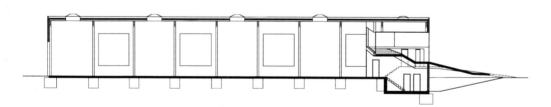

Longitudinal section; views
Längsschnitt; Ansichten

The Elevated Square
Der hochgehobene Platz

The Praterstern in Vienna is a high-rank traffic junction, at once a marked interface within urban space: a star-shaped plaza applied as a joint between the center and the quarters adjacent to the Danube, an intersecting point between a main urban axis line that radiates northward from the center over the Danube and another linking up with the largest green space out of town; finally, this is a topographical and cultural intersection of European stature – the transition from the small-structured central European standard to the open Pannonian Plains and on to the Eurasian spaces. The stellate square has long been dissected by the railroad route and today represents a marginalized interior factor rather than urban space. In a two-stage negotiation procedure, a vision was first sought for the constructional accentuation with 40,000 m^2 of enclosing new buildings and for improved pedestrians' and traffic ways. To a reduced extent, the second step dealt with the remodeling of a railroad station (the intersection of a subway line and routes for commuter trains) with an annexed shopping mall. The central idea of the pool project is to renovate the railroad station square in terms of a roof made passable over ramps and again creating a pedestrian-friendly, nonintersecting and functionally attractive connection between the star's interior and exterior margins.

Der Praterstern in Wien ist ein hochrangiger Verkehrsknoten, zugleich eine markante Schnittstelle im Stadtraum: ein Sternplatz als Gelenk zwischen dem Stadtkern und den an die Donau anschließenden Vierteln, ein Schnittpunkt zwischen einer urbanen Hauptachse, die vom Zentrum über die Donau nach Norden ausstrahlt, und der Hauptachse des größten stadtnahen Grünraums; und schließlich liegt hier gleichsam eine topografische und kulturelle Schnittstelle europäischen Formats – der Übergang vom kleingliedrigen mitteleuropäischen Maß zu den weiteren, offenen Dimensionen der pannonischen Ebene und der eurasischen Räume. Der Sternplatz ist seit langem durch die Bahntrasse zerschnitten und heute eher innere Peripherie als urbaner Raum.
Im zweistufigen Verhandlungsverfahren wurde zunächst eine Vision der baulichen Akzentuierung mit 40.000 m^2 umfassenden Neubauten und Verbesserung aller Weg- und Verkehrsführungen gesucht. Die zweite Stufe behandelte reduziert nur die Neugestaltung des Bahnhofs (Kreuzung von U-Bahn und S-Bahnlinien) mit einem angelagerten Einkaufszentrum. Kernidee des pool-Projekts ist die Neugestaltung des Bahnhofsplatzes als ein von Rampen aus begehbares Dach, das über die Bahntrasse hinweg die inneren und äußeren Ränder des Sterns wieder fußläufig, kreuzungsfrei und auch funktionell attraktiv verbindet.

CAD perspectives: structures; new linking of paths and spaces
Baumassen; Neuverknüpfung der Wege und Räume

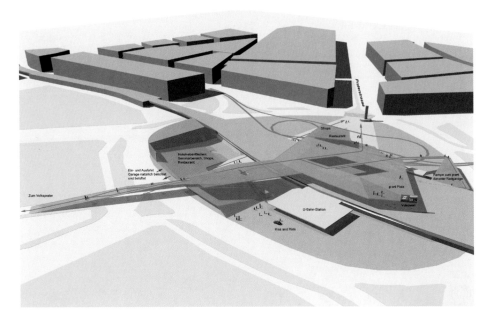

p ort, Vienna Northern Railroad Station – Praterstern
Bahnhof Wien-Nord – Praterstern

ramp

House-and-Town Reticulation
Vernetzung von Haus und Stadt

The project focuses on the corner of a block in downtown Vienna. The building opens inwards to draw in the urban space onto several levels above the access and public functions. Ramps, stairways, office spaces, a restaurant and a lecture hall gather around a complexly modulated space of light. The main access is located at the quayside, below the bar rising up into the first upper floor. Next to the entrance, the space also opens downwards and gives a view into the basement garage. Behind the entrance, set off far into the block's interior, a ramp runs counterwound the garage's departure ramp to access a lounge on the second floor. In turn, the lounge merges into a lecture room that ascends above the restaurant inserted at ground level. The elevators and porter's lodge are deliberately placed into the volume's 'rear' corner; the lecture hall and the bar provide open air spaces above, while their inclines allow sideward perspectives to the docks and the covers of the surrounding office floors. Above the lecture hall, the air space in the other stories is graded up to the southwestern fire wall. The floors' projections and recesses at the quayside, and the projecting ceilings on the southeastern side, provide protection from the sun and invite visitors to step out on the balconies, preventing flashovers and lending the glass façades a body and plasticity.

Das Projekt behandelt eine Blockecke im Zentrum von Wien. Das Gebäude öffnet sich nach innen, zieht über die Erschließung und öffentliche Funktionen den Stadtraum auf mehreren Ebenen ins Innere. Um einen komplex modulierten Raum aus Licht versammeln sich Rampen, Treppen, Büroflächen, Restaurant und ein Auditorium. Der Hauptzugang liegt an der Kai-Seite, unter der sich ins erste Oberge- schoß anhebenden Bar. Neben dem Entree öffnet sich der Raum auch nach unten und gibt Einblick in die Tiefgarage. Hinter dem weit ins Blockinnere zurückgesetzten Eingang führt eine Rampe gegenläufig zur Garagenabfahrt in die Lounge im ersten Stock, die weiter in ein Auditorium übergeht, das im Hauszentrum über dem ebenerdig einge- lagerten Restaurant ansteigt. Lifte und Portier liegen bewusst in der ‚hinteren' Ecke des Volumens; Auditorium und Bar lassen Lufträume nach oben frei und schaffen durch die Schrägen auch seitliche Durch- blicke zum Kai und zum Mantel der umschließenden Büroetagen. Über dem Auditorium staffelt sich der Luftraum in den weiteren Etagen an die südwestliche Feuermauer heran. Die Vor- und Rücksprünge der Geschoße an der Kaiseite und die auskragenden Decken an der Süd- ostseite bieten Sonnenschutz und Austritt auf Balkone, verhindern Brandüberschlag und geben den Glasfassaden Körper und Plastizität.

becomes room

pool

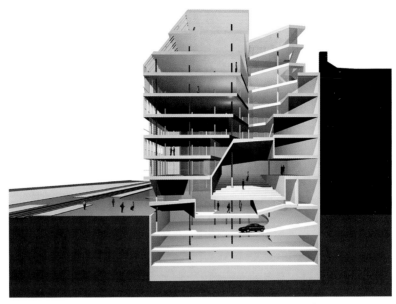

View from quayside; perspective section
Ansicht vom Kai; perspektivischer Schnitt

The property was confronted with legal permissions for two different heights of construction. First, the small section and a part of the area that could be set up to a larger height have been planned to steer clear of any problems once adding an additional story. The office and commercial areas are elevated by roughly one meter above the street level. The parking spaces located below are thus given natural lighting and ventilation. The garage is already calculated for definite requirements, acting to avoid a second garage story that is legally compulsory in the case of higher developments. Counterwound to the departure ramp, an external pedestrians' ramp and an interior staircase lead up to the commercial level. The garage ramp itself is located in the switchyards facing the workshops and is roofed by fliers set up in front of the recess and communication area. Accessible from the entrance hall, these stairs lead up to a roof terrace that can be used as a break room; with a story added, they form the interior connection to the offices on the upper floor.

What Moves the Form
Was die Form bewegt

raumwerdung

Das Grundstück weist zwei unterschiedliche Bauklassen auf. In einem ersten Schritt wird der kleine Abschnitt mit Bauklasse 1 und ein Teil des höher bebaubaren Bereichs so geplant, dass die spätere Aufstockung problemlos ist. Die Büro- und Geschäftsflächen sind um etwa einen Meter gegenüber dem Straßenniveau angehoben. Dadurch erhalten die darunter liegenden Stellplätze natürliche Belichtung und Belüftung. Die Garage ist bereits jetzt für den endgültigen Bedarf bemessen. So wird ein beim höheren Ausbau rechtlich erforderliches, zweites Garagengeschoß vermieden. Gegenläufig zur Abfahrtsrampe führen eine äußere Fußgängerrampe und eine innere Treppe auf das Geschäftsniveau. Die Garagenrampe selbst liegt im Bereich der Rangierflächen vor den Werkstätten und wird durch eine dem Erholungs- und Kommunikationsbereich vorgelagerte Freitreppe überdacht. Vom Foyer aus zugänglich führt diese Treppe auf eine als Pausenraum nutzbare Dachterrasse; bei der Aufstockung bildet sie dann die innere Verbindung zu den Büros im ersten Stock.

View from the street, access
Ansicht von der Straße, Zufahrt

der rampe

pool

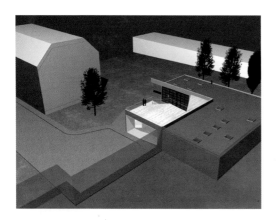

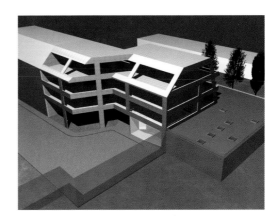

CAD perspectives 1st and 2nd building phases; ground plans
1. und 2. Bauphase; Grundrisse

ramp

Raumplan 2000
Raumplan 2000

The property descends to the north, the building had to be set up along-side an adjacent house to the west, and distance maintained to the street to the south. These parameters transformed its design into an optimum of spatial quality. A cubic theme makes full use of the legally permissible volume. The two floors and a basement are 'modulated' into the slope's inclination such that it offers six usable levels and an abundance of spatial-plastic aspects. An automobile is parked under the main cube in the lower story's indentation, open on its sides, en lieu of a garage. As to the ground plan, as well, the ramp runs in slantingly from the allotment's southeastern corner and under the cube – for reasons of inclination and overhead clearance. In parallel, a footpath leads halfway up the ramp to the entrance. The alignment from the door and forecourt is turned out of its orthogonality in the opposite direction. The hallway itself is only as high and large as necessary, backed by a 'toilet wedge' that is logical in any respect. From there on, and continuing the above twofold inclinations, a whole sequence of staggered levels develops up to the roof terrace and down to the garden. The fully open stairway sculpture is a most concentrated achievement, a modern version of the economy formulated by Loos and Frank, 'providing instead of consuming additional living space'.

Das Grundstück fällt nach Norden, westlich musste an ein Nachbarhaus angebaut werden, im Süden war Distanz zur Straße zu halten. Diese Parameter transformiert der Entwurf zu einem Optimum an Raum-qualität. Das rechtlich mögliche Volumen ist als kubische Grundform ausgereizt. Die zwei Etagen mit einem Sockelgeschoß sind so in die Hangneigung ‚moduliert' und als Konsequenz daraus ist der Kubus so frei manipuliert, dass er sechs nutzbare Ebenen und eine Fülle an räumlich-plastischen Aspekten bietet. Statt in einer Garage wird der PKW unter dem Hauptkubus in der seitlich offenen Einbuchtung des Untergeschoßes geparkt. Die Rampe läuft vom Südosteck der Parzelle auch grundrisslich schief unter den Kubus hinein – aus Gründen der Neigung und Durchfahrtshöhe. Parallel dazu führt der Fußweg auf halber Höhe der Rampe zum Eingang. Die Flucht von Tür und Vorplatz ist in die Gegenrichtung aus der Orthogonalität gedreht. Das Entree selbst ist nur so hoch und groß wie nötig, mit dem in jeder Hinsicht logischen ‚Klokeil' im Rücken. In Fortsetzung der genannten zwei-fachen Schrägen entwickelt sich nun von da aus die ganze Sequenz der versetzten Ebenen hinauf bis zur Dachterrasse, hinunter zum Garten. Die allseits offene Treppenskulptur ist konzentrierteste Leistungsform, eine moderne Version der von Loos und Frank formulierten Ökonomie, bietet ‚zusätzlichen Wohnraum, anstatt ihn zu verbrauchen'.

Vista from the street into the green
Durchblick von der Straße zum Grün

becomes room

House in spe
Haus in spe

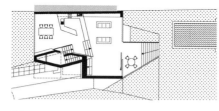

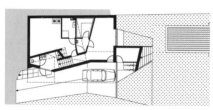

Ground plans; detail stairways; garden side
Grundrisse; Detail Stiege; Gartenseite

pool
Weyringergasse 36/1, A–1040 Wien
Tel +43-1-503 82 31-0, Fax +43-1-503 82 31-33
pool@helma.at, www.pool.helma.at

Christoph Lammerhuber, Axel Linemayr, Florian Wallnöfer and **Evelyn Rudnicki** are pool. They have been collaborating since 1993 and founded pool Architektur ZT GmbH in 1998.
Buildings, projects (select): House in spe, Vienna, 1998–99; T.O. Penthouse, Vienna, 1999; trum, Locksmith's Hall and Bar, Trumau, Lower Austria (2000 Austrian Clients Prize), 1998–2000; pc, Office Building, Vienna, 1999–2000; rolphi, Sunglasses Shop, Wiener Neudorf, Lower Austria, 2000; ZOOM Kids' Museum, Vienna, 2001; mcs, Office and Commercial Building, Vienna; Einöde House, Pfaffstätten, Lower Austria, both 2000–02. Under construction: mom, Attic Extension, Vienna. Planned: AMZ, Office Building; Kabelwerk Residential Dwellings; nugget, Residential and Office Building; all in Vienna. Competitions (select): bel-m, KDAG Grounds, Vienna, 1998; sehr gut, Vienna Primary School, 1998; lgkfld, Innsbruck Administration Building, 1999; sara, Sarajevo Concert Hall, 1999; kölnice, Cologne ICE-Terminal, 1999; kuga, Kunsthaus Graz, 2000; satz, Exhibition Center, Salzburg, 2000; bop mester, Budapest Business Park, 2001; okai, Office Building, Vienna, 2001; p ort, Vienna Northern Railroad Station – Praterstern, 2001–02.

Christoph Lammerhuber, Axel Linemayr, Florian Wallnöfer und **Evelyn Rudnicki** sind pool. Sie arbeiten seit 1993 zusammen, 1998 gründeten sie die pool Architektur ZT GmbH.
Bauten, Projekte (Auswahl): 1998–99 Haus in spe, Wien; 1999 T.O. Penthouse, Wien; 1998–2000 trum, Schlosserhalle mit Bar, Trumau, NÖ (Bauherrenpreis Österreich 2000); 1999–2000 Bürogebäude pc, Wien; 2000 rolphi, Shop für Sonnenbrillen, Wiener Neudorf, NÖ; 2001 Kindermuseum ZOOM, Wien; 2000–02 mcs, Büro- und Geschäftsgebäude, Wien; Haus Einöde, Pfaffstätten, NÖ. In Bau: Dachbodenausbau mom, Wien. In Planung: Bürogebäude AMZ; Wohnbauten Kabelwerk; Wohn- und Bürogebäude nugget; alle Wien. Wettbewerbe (Auswahl): 1998 bel-m, KDAG-Gründe, Wien; 1998 sehr gut, Volksschule Wien; 1999 lgkfld, Verwaltungsgebäude Innsbruck; 1999 sara, Konzerthalle Sarajewo; 1999 kölnice, ICE-Terminal Köln; 2000 kuga, Kunsthaus Graz; 2000 satz, Ausstellungszentrum, Salzburg; 2001 bop mester, Business Park Budapest; 2001 okai, Bürogebäude, Wien; 2001–02 p ort, Bahnhof Wien-Nord – Praterstern.

House in spe / Haus in spe, Wien
Client / Bauherr: Ulrike Hoschek-Ginner and / und Robert Grischany
Statics / Statik: Fröhlich & Locher
Building contractors / Bauunternehmen: Fa. Jägerbau
Glasswork / Glasarbeiten: Fa. Alutechnik

bel-m, KDAG Grounds, competition / KDAG-Gründe, Wien, Wettbewerb
Client / Bauherr: Magistrat der Stadt Wien, MA 21B, and / und Kabelwerk GmbH
Consultant / Konsulent: Manfred Schenekl

trum, Locksmith's Hall and Bar / Schlosserhalle mit Bar, Trumau
Client / Bauherr: Uschi and / und Ernst Hofmann
Statics / Statik: Fröhlich & Locher
Structural steelwork / Konstruktiver Stahlbau: Fa. Scholl
Cladding and metalworks / Fassade und Schlosserarbeiten: Fa. Hofmann

p ort, Vienna Northern Railroad Station – Praterstern, competition / Bahnhof Wien-Nord –
Praterstern, Wettbewerb
Project partner / Projektpartner: Hans Lechner ZT GmbH
Client / Bauherr: Austrian Federal Railroads / Österreichische Bundesbahnen
Collaborator / Mitarbeiter: Benjamin Konrad
Statics / Statik: Fröhlich & Locher
Consultant / Konsulent: Manfred Schenekl

okai, Office Building, competition / Bürogebäude, Wien, Wettbewerb
Client / Bauherr: Zürich Kosmos Versicherungen AG
Consultant / Konsulent: Manfred Schenekl

mcs, Office and Commercial Building / Büro- und Geschäftsgebäude, Wien
Client / Bauherr: Johann Slauf
Collaborators / Mitarbeiter: Alexa Zahn, Benjamin Konrad
Statics / Statik: Werkraum Wien
Building contractor / Bauunternehmen: Fa. Leitzinger
Electrical and service contractor / Elektro- und HLS-Installationen: Fa. Sanda
Glasswork / Glasarbeiten: Fa. Planer

Architekturzentrum Wien; Springer-Verlag Wien New York; Text: © Otto Kapfinger
Photo credits: © by the architects and: Hertha Hurnaus: 109, 111, 115–117, 125–127, 129, 130

PPAG Anna Popelka Georg Poduschka

Knights of the 3-D Chessboard
Springer im Raum-Schach

Chess is the infinite potentiality of strategic constellations on a grid field. Knights are not the most powerful, yet perhaps the most dynamic chess pieces. Unlike other actors, they advance into the third dimension while clearing pieces in front and may move around with short darts to as many as eight different squares. The spatial quality in PPAG's architecture unfolds from similar moves vaulting to exceed the conventional zonings of surfaces and levels. Their buildings show horizontally and vertically flexed sectional areas. The L-forms are either packed into one another in a mirrored fashion or arranged in spirals around a midline. Spatial structure is also created subtractively, meandering ways both hollowing out and unlocking a given volume. Ever since the early 1990s, PPAG have produced complex cuts and surprising spatial sequences based on the simplest of geometries. Their spatial loops developed independently from the foldings, splicings or interweavings of surfaces associated with a fashion that has since come to be rife. In 1993/94, apartment projects by Georg Poduschka already showed vertical meanders and innovative modes of circulation. In 1994, Anna Popelka developed the series of 'residential models': Studies involving height-staggered and out-of-center elements or small hooked modules that virtually produced molecular proliferations when added and varied on all sides. In 1995, PPAG 'deconstructed' the prism of the Vienna norm

Schachspiel ist die unendliche Möglichkeit strategischer Konstellationen auf dem Rasterfeld. Nicht die mächtigste, vielleicht die dynamischste Figur ist der Springer. Im Gegensatz zu den anderen Akteuren stößt er in die dritte Dimension vor. Er kann die vor ihm postierten Figuren überspringen und mit kurzen Haken acht Felder im Umkreis erreichen. Die Raumqualität in der Architektur von PPAG entsteht aus ähnlichen Spielzügen, die im Rösselsprung über konventionelle Zonierungen von Flächen und Etagen hinausgehen. Ihre Gebäude zeigen horizontal und vertikal abgewinkelte Schnittflächen. Die L-Formen sind entweder gespiegelt ineinandergepackt oder in Spiralen um eine Mittelachse gruppiert. Es gibt aber auch die subtraktive Erzeugung des Raumgefüges, indem ein vorgegebenes Volumen durch mäandrierende Wege innerlich ausgehöhlt und zugleich aufgeschlossen wird. Komplexe Schnitte und überraschende Raumfolgen auf der Basis einfachster Geometrien gibt es bei PPAG seit den frühen neunziger Jahren. Ihre Raumschleifen entstanden unabhängig von der inzwischen grassierenden Mode der Faltung, Spleißung oder Verwebung von Flächen. Schon 1993/94 plante Georg Poduschka bei Wohnbauprojekten vertikale Mäander und innovative Erschließungsformen. 1994 entwickelte Anna Popelka die Serie der ‚Wohnmodelle': Etüden mit zueinander höhen- und seitenversetzten Elementen oder mit kleinen Haken-Modulen, die nach allen

Praterstraße Housing, Vienna
Wohnbau Praterstraße

classroom, simply by isolating and grading above glass corridor enfilades – with the result of a novel type of school. This was followed by a constructed vertical apartment meander in Vienna's Praterstraße, the vertical rotation of L-rooms at the Stadtvilla in Linz, and the counterbore of a minimized block, by an oscillating movement of corridors and air spaces, with the project for the Eisenstadt City Hall. PPAG play three-dimensional chess according to simple rules. Maximized spatial potential is to be accompanied by minimized expenditures. The procedures are far from any constructive or formal excesses. 'Architecture is not an art,' they say, 'but a science' – a science investigating complex patterns of simple basic elements, defining urban volumes from surrounding factors, breaking down such data sculptures with the tools of space chess. PPAG are 'not in love with thin supports, accept the datum such as gravity, working on sensation in all similitude.'

Seiten addiert und variiert gleichsam molekulare Wucherungen erzeugten. 1995 ‚dekonstruierten' PPAG das Prisma der Wiener Normklasse durch bloße Isolation und Staffelung über gläsernen Gangfluchten zu einem neuartigen Schultypus. Es folgte der gebaute, vertikale Wohnungs-mäander in der Praterstraße, die vertikale Rotation der L-Räume bei der Stadtvilla für Linz und die Aufbohrung eines minimierten Baublocks durch pendelnde Bewegung von Fluren und Lufträumen beim Projekt für das Rathaus Eisenstadt. PPAG spielen Raumschach nach einfachen Regeln. Maximierung des Raumpotenzials und Minimierung des Aufwands ist angesagt. Konstruktive oder formale Exzesse liegen da fern. ‚Architektur ist keine Kunst', sagen sie, ‚sondern eine Wissenschaft' – der komplexen Baumuster aus simplen Grundelementen, der Definition urbaner Volumina aus den Faktoren der Umgebung, der Aufgliederung solcher Datenskulpturen mit den Werkzeugen des Raumschachs. PPAG sind ‚nicht verliebt in dünne Stützen, nehmen das Gegebene wie die Schwerkraft, arbeiten an der Sensation in aller Ähnlichkeit'.

Electric Avenue, MuseumsQuartier, Vienna
Electric Avenue, MuseumsQuartier

raum ist

The quiet backyard allowed for a volume of 21 m by 6 m and 18 m high.
PPAG tailored this volume into a meandered stratification of space.
Six floors would normally have been developed here, but PPAG realized
seven. They divided the prism into boundary fields and a center zone,
5 m and 11 m in width, resp. The room heights were pressed down
to the permitted minimum of 2.2 m in the latter zone, and the building
height could thus be divided in sevenths. The elevator and stairways
are located on the north side, and sanitary rooms, the kitchen zones and
generous lobbies (to be used as bedrooms, as well) on the south.
In turn, the stories' eastern and western margins offer rooms set lower
or higher by five steps and showing a floor-to-floor height of 3.2 m.
Varying Le Corbusier's 'Unité' type, PPAG upset the hook modules to one
and a half stories, let the long and low leg be half-clasped by the next
unit's short, high leg, and swiveled the system from the building's cross
section into the longitudinal section. Complemented by balconies and
a roof terrace, a multiply useable spatial structure develops to show
distinct tensions between wide and low, high and deep dimensions. As
to typology of space, the innovation is technically simple and converted
without further ado along standards that are affordable in apartment
house building.

Vertical Meander
Vertikaler Mäander

Im ruhigen Hinterhof war ein Bauvolumen von 21 m Breite, 6 m Tiefe
und 18m Höhe erlaubt. PPAG formten daraus eine maßgeschneiderte,
mäandrierende Raumschichtung. Im Normalfall wären hier sechs
Etagen entstanden, PPAG erzielten aber sieben Wohnebenen. Sie teilten
das Prisma in 5 m breite Randfelder und eine 11 m breite Mittelzone.
In dieser wurden die Raumhöhen auf das erlaubte Mindestmaß von
2,2 m gedrückt, was die Sieben-Teilung der Bauhöhe ermöglichte. Hier
liegen nordseitig Lift und Stiege, südseitig Nassräume, Küchenzone und
großzügige Dielen (auch als Schlafräume nutzbar); die Ost- und
Westränder der Etagen bieten dagegen um fünf Stufen tiefer- bzw. höher-
gesetzte Räume mit 3,2 m Plafondhöhe. Den Typus der ‚Unité'
von Le Corbusier variierend, stauchen PPAG die Haken-Module auf
eineinhalb Geschoße, lassen den langen, niederen Schenkel halb vom
kurzen, hohen der nächsten Einheit umgreifen und schwenken das
System vom Quer- in den Längsschnitt des Gebäudes. Ergänzt mit
Balkonen und Dachterrasse entsteht ein vielfältig nutzbares Raumgefüge
mit starken Spannungen zwischen breit und niedrig, hoch und tief.
Die raumtypologische Innovation ist technisch simpel und ohne Um-
schweife mit den im Miethausbau leistbaren Standards umgesetzt.

Living room with a difference of level, kitchen pulpit
Wohnraum mit Niveausprung, Küchenkanzel

überfunktiona

Dense package, change in interior dimensions
Dichte Packung, Dimensionswechsel im Inneren

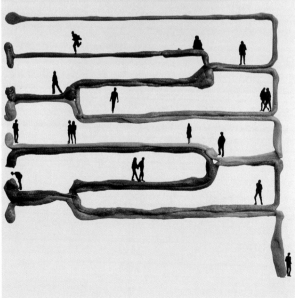

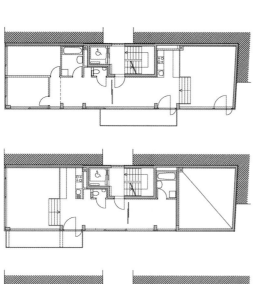

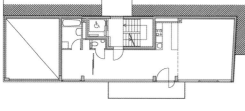

Model; ground plans; stairs up to the roof terrace
Modell; Grundrisse; Treppe zur Dachterrasse

absurdes

Silver-Clad, High-Tech Leviathan
Hightech-Leviathan im Silbermantel

The testing plant in Floridsdorf, Vienna, provided another approach for PPAG's 'space chess'. Two wind tunnels 30 and 100 m in length are able to simulate any climate given on earth and generate wind speeds up to 250 km/h. The plant tests the most modern railroad trains, subways, busses and magnetic cushion trains. Unique in Europe, it is complemented by preparation halls, refrigeration facilities, transformer wings, offices, and service and controlling zones. The architects arranged the technical units located on the narrow site into a linear structure that was open for change already anticipated in the course of the planning and assembly phases. Two key creative issues were approached in collaboration with international specialist planners. The first was to organize the spatial allocation of the individual, autonomous and high-determined individual areas. Secondly, use was to be made of the interspaces between the plant's components and the interstices between the enormous wind tunnel pipes and the shells – in terms of paths and bridges, views and vistas in connection with lobbies and office surfaces. Another aspect touched upon the shell's design as a homogeneous, silvery form that subordinates all individual functions to a large entity and stages the project's dimension. Signal-like tints mark the interior together with the interplay between 'hard' engineering zones and 'soft' human zones.

Einen anderen Ansatz für das ‚Raum-Schach‘ von PPAG bot die Test-anlage in Wien-Floridsdorf. Zwei Windkanäle mit 30 und 100 m Länge können jedes auf der Erde gegebene Klima simulieren und Wind-geschwindigkeiten bis 250 km/h erzeugen. Man testet hier modernste Zuggarnituren, U-Bahnen, Busse oder Magnetschwebebahnen. Die in Europa einmalige Anlage wird durch Vorbereitungshallen, Kühlanlagen, Transformatorentrakt, Büroräume sowie Service- und Kontrollzonen ergänzt. Die Architekten ordneten die technischen Einheiten auf dem schmalen Bauplatz zu einer linearen Struktur, offen für Veränderungen, die noch während der Planung und Montage zu erwarten waren. In Kooperation mit internationalen Spezialplanern gab es zwei gestalterische Hauptthemen: die räumliche Zuordnung der autonomen, hochdeter-minierten Einzelbereiche zu organisieren und die Zwischenräume zwischen den Anlageteilen, die ‚Schluffe‘ zwischen den riesigen Wind-kanalröhren und den Gebäudehüllen zu nutzen für Wegführungen und Brücken, für Ein- und Durchblicke in Verbindung mit Foyers und Büroflächen. Ein anderer Aspekt betraf das Design der Bauhülle als homogene, silberglänzende Form, die alle Einzelfunktionen einem großen Ganzen unterordnet und die Dimension des Projekts in Szene setzt. Signalhafte Farbakzente und das Spiel zwischen ‚harten‘ Technik-zonen und ‚weichen‘ Humanzonen prägen das Innere.

Lobby, vista to the wind tunnel; instruction room
Foyer, Durchblick zum Windkanal; Schulungsraum

ist startpunkt

Lobby; corridor on the upper floor office wing
Foyer; Flur im Obergeschoß Bürotrakt

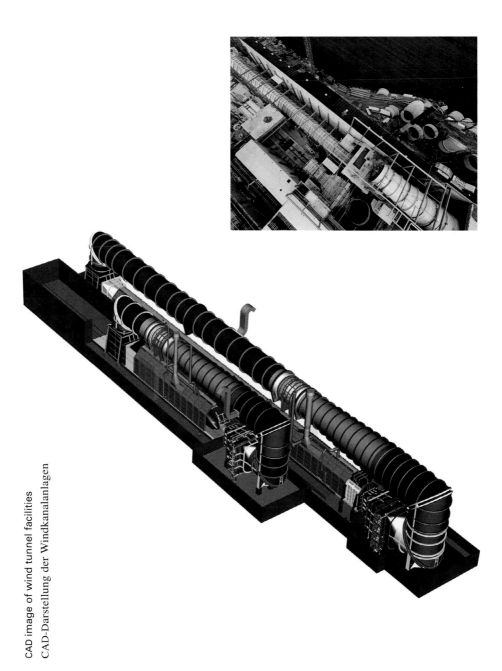

CAD image of wind tunnel facilities
CAD-Darstellung der Windkanalanlagen

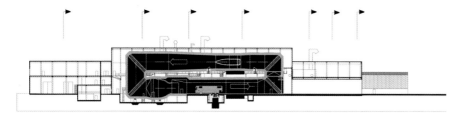

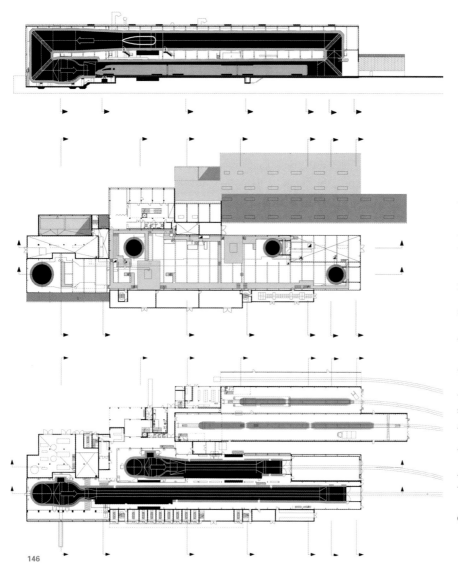

Ground plans; longitudinal sections of small and large wind tunnel
Grundrisse; Längsschnitte großer und kleiner Windkanal

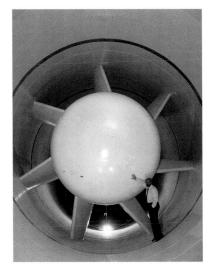

Construction; in the tunnel; fan
Konstruktion; im Kanal; Gebläse

space

A Block as a Data Sculpture
Baublock als Datenskulptur

On a larger scale, PPAG's disposition finds its conclusion in an urbanistic approach. Here, too, they address given restraints offensively, transform the data gathered from building codes, light-shadow diagrams, local free space qualities and stipulated distances to surrounding buildings into precise envelopes of possible developments to cover the area. PPAG, void of typological bias, thus develop a 'data sculpture' with a maximum free space of interior differentiation. Free from care, they leave behind the classic patterns of unit constructions or point block building, as much as the old figure-ground debate. After the first competition project of this kind for Graz, the approach brought PPAG first prize in the 6ᵗʰ Europan competition for a plot in Vienna. Like the 'datascapes' developed in Holland, they define urban blocks of building as artificial mountains into which the claims of the environs are primarily inscribed: the interior ways, inner effects of surrounding free spaces, and the lighting of the deeper zones altogether dig incisions, form plazas upon which private and public life may mix, as well as residential action and other occupancies. A quote from the jury: 'The project opens a discussion space to surround the urban block and its possible transformation. It makes the issue of feasibility the method of design.'

Im städtebaulichen Ansatz findet die Haltung von PPAG ihre Konsequenz im größeren Maßstab. Auch hier gehen sie offensiv auf gegebene Zwänge zu, transformieren sie die Daten der Bauordnung, der Licht-Schattendiagramme, der lokalen Freiraumqualitäten und der Abstandsregeln zu den Umgebungsbauten in präzise Hüllkurven möglicher Bebauung über dem Areal. So entwickeln sie ohne typologische Befangenheit eine ‚Datenskulptur' mit maximalem Freiraum der inneren Differenzierung und lassen die klassischen Muster der Block- oder Punktbebauung, aber auch die alte Figur-Grund-Debatte ohne viel Federlesens hinter sich. Nach einem ersten Wettbewerbsprojekt dieser Art für Graz konnten PPAG den 6. Europan-Bewerb für ein Grundstück in Wien mit dieser Methode gewinnen. Den in Holland entwickelten ‚datascapes' vergleichbar, definieren sie urbane Baublöcke als künstliche Berge, in die sich primär die Ansprüche der Umgebung einschreiben: die inneren Wege, die internen Auswirkungen der umgebenden Freiräume und die Belichtung der tieferen Zonen graben Einschnitte, bilden Plazas, an denen sich privates und öffentliches Leben mischen, Wohnen mit anderen Nutzungen koppeln kann. Juryzitat: ‚Das Projekt eröffnet einen Diskussionsraum über den städtischen Block und seine mögliche Transformation. Es macht die Frage der Machbarkeit zur Entwurfsmethode.'

Development of optimal massive structure
Entwicklung der optimalen Baumasse

is hyperfunctional

PPAG Anna Popelka Georg Poduschka

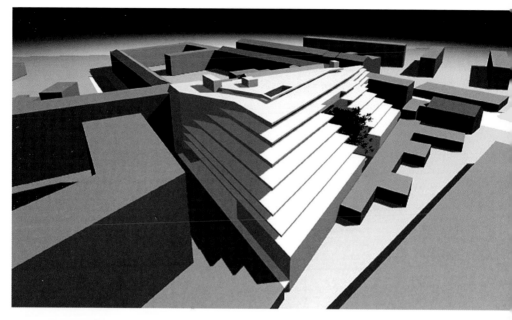

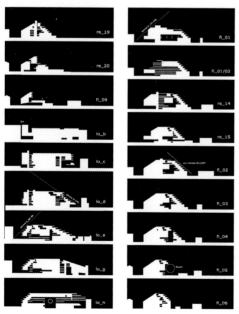

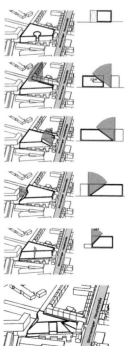

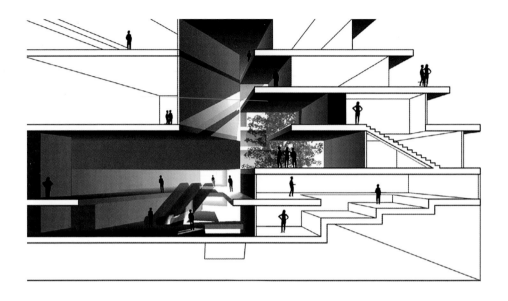

Spatial dissection of the data sculpture
Räumliche Zergliederung der Datenskulptur

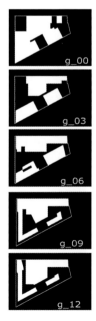

g_00

g_03

g_06

g_09

g_12

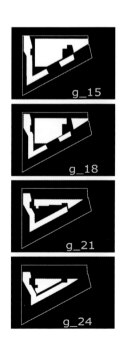

g_15

g_18

g_21

g_24

normalität

Dancing Pergola
Tanzende Pergola

The baroque tunnel vault of the Fischer von Erlach wing at the Wiener MuseumsQuartier was given installations for various occupancies, at once defining and stimulating a public walk. The spatial requirements include record shops, smaller-size offices and a discussion lounge for electronic music. Forced by the Preservation Office to stay aloof of the walls, the gallery zigzags through the halls. The construction reacts to the rhythm of the old building's niches and windows, forges ahead to the light in the lunettes, sways back to the vaults' dark zones. The rhythm also covers the new glass walls along the passageways, from the forecourt to the inner court. Coated in silver, the 'large furnishing' is paned in part and the units are flexible for occupancy. The ephemeral implant varies and precisely outplays the axial quality of the old building. In spite of the interior densification, the old tunnel vaults remain omnipresent and, at street level, for the first time open a passageway along the entire longitudinal axis. Electric Avenue is a dance of today through baroque space, a modern pergola with transitory occupancies, oscillating in the vault's duct between light and dark, above and below.

Das barocke Tonnengewölbe des Fischer von Erlach-Trakts im Wiener MuseumsQuartier erhält Einbauten für verschiedene Nutzungen, die zugleich eine öffentliche Flaniermeile definieren und stimulieren. Die räumlichen Anforderungen reichen vom Plattenladen, kleineren Büroflächen bis zur Diskussions-Lounge für elektronische Musik. Vom Denkmalamt zum Abstand vom Gemäuer gezwungen, zieht sich die Galerie in Zick-Zack-Bewegungen durch die Hallen. Die Konstruktion reagiert auf den Rhythmus der Nischen und Fenster des Altbaus, dringt zum Licht in die Stichkappen vor, schwingt bei den Dunkelzonen der Gewölbe zurück. Auch die neuen Glaswände an den Durchgängen vom Vorplatz zum Innenhof sind in den Rhythmus einbezogen. Das silbrig beschichtete ‚Großmöbel' ist partiell verglast, die nutzbaren Einheiten sind flexibel. Die achsiale Qualität des Altbaus wird durch das ephemere Implantat variiert und präzise überspielt. Trotz der inneren Verdichtung bleiben die alten Tonnengewölbe omnipräsent und eröffnen auf Straßenniveau erstmals den Durchgang in der gesamten Längsachse. Electric Avenue ist der Tanz der Gegenwart durch den barocken Raum, eine moderne Pergola mit transitorischen Nutzungen, im Gewölbekanal oszillierend zwischen licht und dunkel, unten und oben.

Views of the upper level for offices, studios
Ansichten der oberen Ebene für Büros, Studios

wird erreicht

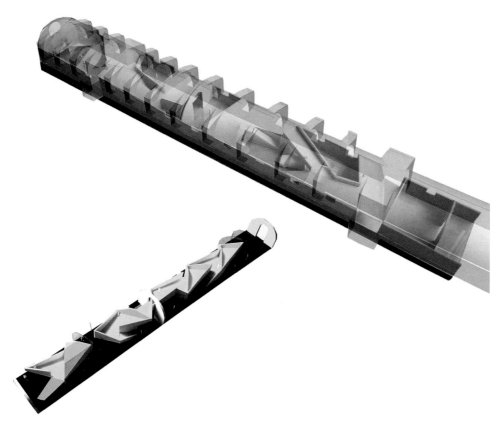

Penetration old – new; CAD perspectives
Durchdringung alt – neu; CAD-Perspektiven

PPAG Anna Popelka Georg Poduschka
Schadekgasse 16/1, A–1060 Wien
Tel +43-1-587 44 71, Fax +43-1-587 44 71
po_po@chello.at, www.ppag.at

Anna Popelka and **Georg Poduschka,** studied architecture from 1980–87 at the TU in Graz, and from 1986–94 at the TU in Graz as well as the Ecole d'Architecture Paris-Tolbiac. Upper Austrian Promotion Prize; Viennese Promotion Prize 1994. PPAG Anna Popelka Georg Poduschka since 1995. Visiting professorship in 1997/98 at the Department of Interior Design, Vienna TU.

Buildings, projects (select): Praterstraße Housing and Attic Extension, Vienna (1999 Arce Prize), 1995–98; Floatingtank at the Museum of Perception, Graz, 1997–99; Augarten Nord Graz Development Plan Design, competition, 2000. Schadekgasse, PPAG Office and Apartment, 2000; Climatic Wind Tunnel, 2000–02; Electric Avenue/quartier21, MuseumsQuartier, 2001–02; all in Vienna. Planned: Glanzinggasse Housing (competition, 1st prize), 1999; Europan 6 (competition, 1st prize), 2001; all in Vienna. Rosenauerstraße Housing, Linz, 2002–05.

Exhibitions, lectures, publications: The Scent of Architecture, Moscow, Venice, Buenos Aires, Budapest, Vienna, 1998–2000; Young European Architects, Biennale di Venezia and Buenos Aires, 2000; Lectures at the MIT, Cambridge, and ESARQ Barcelona in 2000; University of Applied Arts Vienna 2000; PPAG – Das Buch (2 volumes), 2001/02.

Anna Popelka und **Georg Poduschka,** 1980–87 Architekturstudium an der TU Graz bzw. 1986–94 Architekturstudium an der TU Graz und an der Ecole d'Architecture Paris-Tolbiac. 1994 Förderungspreis des Landes OÖ, des Landes Wien. Seit 1995 PPAG Anna Popelka Georg Poduschka. WS 1997/98 Gastprofessur am Institut für Raumgestaltung der TU Wien.

Bauten, Projekte (Auswahl): 1995–98 Praterstraße Wohnbau und Dachausbau, Wien (Arce Preis 1999); 1997–99 Floatingtank im Museum der Wahrnehmung, Graz; 2000 Bebauungsplanentwurf Augarten Nord Graz, Wettbewerb; 2000 Schadekgasse, eigenes Büro und Wohnung; 2000–02 Klimawindkanal; 2001–02 Electric Avenue / quartier 21, MuseumsQuartier; alle Wien. In Planung: 1999 Wohnbau Glanzinggasse (Wettbewerb, 1. Preis); 2001 Europan 6 (Wettbewerb, 1. Preis); alle Wien. 2002–05 Wohnbau Rosenauerstraße, Linz.

Ausstellungen, Vorträge, Publikationen: 1998–2000 The Scent of Architecture, Moskau, Venedig, Buenos Aires, Budapest, Wien; 2000 Young European Architects, Biennale di Venezia und Buenos Aires; 2000 Vorträge am MIT, Cambridge, und ESARQ Barcelona; Universität für angewandte Kunst, Wien; 2001/02 PPAG – Das Buch (2 Bände).

Praterstraße Housing and Attic Extension, direct commission / Wohnbau und Dachausbau, Direktauftrag, Wien 2
Client / Bauherr: CONWERT GesmbH
Constructional physics / Bauphysik: Reiner Rothbacher, Zell am See
Building inspection, chief technical-executive management / Bauaufsicht, technisch-geschäftliche Oberleitung: Arch. Heinz Lutter
Collaborators / Mitarbeiter PPAG: Christine Bärnthaler, Jutta Gössler, Andreas Kurzböck
Statics / Statik: Herbert Endl, Wien

Electric Avenue / quartier21, experts selection project / Electric Avenue / quartier21, Gutachterprojekt, MuseumsQuartier Wien
Client / Bauherr: Museumsquartier Errichtungs- und Betriebsges.m.b.H.
Concept / Konzept quartier21: Vitus H. Weh
Project management / Projektmanagement: Bergsmann pm, Katzelsdorf
Acoustics / Akustik: Quiring Consultants, Innsbruck
Collaborators / Mitarbeiter: Klaus Moldan, Maik Novotny, Corinna Toell
Statics / Statik: Fritsch Chiari & Partner, Wien
Structural steelwork / Stahlbau: MCE VOEST GmbH & Co

Climatic Wind Tunnel, total entrepreneur competition / Klimawindkanal, Wien 21, Totalunternehmerverfahren
Building and holding company / Errichtungs- und Besitzgesellschaft: Rail Test & Research GesmbH
Building consultant / Consultant des Errichters: Ingenieurgemeinschaft Klima-Wind-Kanal Wien
Operating company / Betriebsgesellschaft: Rail Tec Arsenal GesmbH
Total entrepreneur / Totalunternehmer: Arbeitsgemeinschaft Klima-Wind-Kanal Wien AIOLOS – VA MCE – ELIN EBG
Central management / Federführung: MCE VOEST GmbH & Co
General planner, statics massive construction / Generalplaner, Statik Massivbau: Bautechnik Linz Planungsgesellschaft m.b.H.
Collaborators / Mitarbeiter: Christine Bärnthaler, Tobias Hanig, Sebastian Illichmann, Klaus Moldan, Maik Novotny, Madeleine Ozdoba, Silvia Panek, Isabella Strauss, Titusz Tarnai, Corinna Toell, Aleks Torbica
Other involved companies / Weitere beteiligte Firmen: Aiolos Engineering Corporation, Toronto; Axima Refrigeration GmbH, Lindau; Voith Howden GmbH, Heidenheim; Voest Alpine Industrieanlagenbau GmbH & Co; Praher Schuster ZT GmbH; Logistik Service GmbH, Linz; Dynamotive Ltd., Leicestershire, UK; IBS, Institut für Brandschutztechnik und Sicherungsforschung Gesellschaft m.b.H.; TAS Schreiner GmbH, Linz

Europan 6, competition, 1st prize / Europan 6, Wettbewerb, 1. Preis, Wien 10
Client / Bauherr: Mischek / Wiener Heim Wohnbauges.m.b.H.
Collaborators / Mitarbeiter: Klaus Moldan, Maik Novotny, Nick Stüzle
Statics / Statik: Mischek ZT GmbH

Architekturzentrum Wien; Springer-Verlag Wien New York; Text: © Otto Kapfinger
Photo credits: © by the architects and: a+t: 140; Christine Bärnthaler: 133, 137, 141, 153, 154; Manfred Burger: 147; Julia Oppermann: 139; Peter Pauer/MCE Voest: 145, 147; Studio Krauss: 135, 140, 141, 143, 144, 147

RATAPLAN

their career typifies those of the new viennese groups. the five team members started out into self-employment right after their studies, without years of acquiring experience in architects' offices. their first jobs included interior design and conversions for NPOs, for agencies in commercial design, the media, fashion. the maxims they developed from the very beginnings applied to collectivity, role-swapping and equal rights in each stage of work, from designing to supervising construction. everybody does everything, there are no specializations. the office is deliberately held 'small' in an attempt to maintain the intensity of internal communication and to offer clients a compact, flexible vis-à-vis. the office is considered a key living space, and working-time quality of life is given much attention. for instance, every member of the team enjoys three months of vacation privileges, and RATAPLAN organized their own insurance without consulting professional associations. quite logical then, but no matter of course, that such rejection of conventional job descriptions would lead to political involvement: RATAPLAN are among the proponents and activists of the ig architektur, founded in vienna as an alternative to the chamber of architecture. they consider the equilibrium 'between individuality and anonymity', pure work with novel and with economical materials, and the level of details withdrawn to a unpretentious and unproblematic plane to formulate a creative

ihre karriere ist typisch für die neuen wiener gruppen. die fünf teammitglieder starteten nach dem studium sofort in die selbständigkeit, ohne praxisjahre in architekturbüros. die ersten jobs waren innenausstattungen und umbauten für NPOs, für agenturen aus den bereichen grafik, medien, mode. kollektivität, rollentausch und gleichberechtigung in jeder arbeitsphase, vom entwurf bis zur bauaufsicht, waren von beginn an maximen. alle tun alles, es gibt keine spezialisierung. das büro wird bewusst ‚klein' gehalten, um die intensität der internen kommunikation zu erhalten und den auftraggebern ein kompaktes, flexibles vis-à-vis zu bieten. das büro wird als wesentlicher lebensraum aufgefasst. der lebensqualität der arbeitszeit wird viel beachtung geschenkt. so hat jedes teammitglied einen jährlichen anspruch auf drei urlaubsmonate, und abseits der professionellen verbände organisierte man sich auch die eigene versicherung. logisch, aber nicht selbstverständlich, dass solche abkehr vom überkommenen berufsbild auch zum politischen engagement führte: RATAPLAN zählt zu den proponenten und aktivisten der in wien alternativ zur architektenkammer gegründeten ig architektur. als eine gestalterische konsequenz der teamstruktur sehen sie die balance ‚zwischen individualität und anonymität', das pure arbeiten mit neuen, mit ökonomischen materialien, das zurücknehmen der detailebene ins unprätentiöse und unproblematische.

AFS1, housing, vienna
AFS1, wohnbau

conclusion arising from the team's structure. they show particular care with respect to 'invisible' design – in ways guided, connections, zoning in space, channeling light, in keeping commitments open for the benefit of spontaneous and accumulated development. with a seldom-encountered degree of intensity, they devote themselves to the ground's tural condition, often underestimated. their free-standing shear walls and screens set in front of existing walls act syntactically and syncopatively with regard to the grounds' organization. while the horizontal regulates the movement and distribution – the interplay between ways and places – the verticals act as view filters and containers, as sculptors of light and molders of moods. quite like in the case of minimalist theater or performance spaces, their architecture concentrates on such interdependence between the horizontal and the vertical, on uninterrupted stage-floor choreographies that are superposed and dramatized by the setting of vertical abutment pieces – polyvalent screens that differentiate, emotionalize space with substantial and functional laminations. unlike examples of a 'design of desire', increasingly limited to merely staging themselves, RATAPLAN always keeps to the timing in an intermediate zone where sensuality may subtly flash through and sobriety is accepted as a horizon and a background.

besondere sorgfalt zeigen sie im ‚unsichtbaren' designbereich – in der wegführung, verknüpfung, zonierung von raum, in der lichtführung, im offenhalten von festlegungen für die anlagerung spontaner entwicklung. mit selten anzutreffender intensität widmen sie sich dem stoff, dem klang, den texturen und rhythmen des bodens – des bodens als der primären kondition von architektur, die zumeist unterschätzt wird. syntaktisch und synkopisch zur organisation der böden agieren ihre freistehenden wandscheiben oder die den bestehenden mauern vorgesetzten screens. regelt die horizontale die bewegung und verteilung – das spiel zwischen wegen und plätzen –, so wirken die vertikalen als sichtfilter und container, als licht- und stimmungsbildner. wie im minimalistischen raum von theater oder performance konzentriert sich ihre architektur auf diese interdependenz von horizontal und vertikal, auf die durchgehende choreografie des (bühnen)bodens, überlagert und dramatisiert durch die setzung vertikaler schwellen – polyvalenter paravents, die den raum mit inhaltlichen und funktionellen schichtungen differenzieren, emotionalisieren. im unterschied zu beispielen, wo das ‚design des begehrens' nur mehr sich selbst inszeniert, bleibt RATAPLAN stets im timing, in jener zwischenzone, wo sinnlichkeit subtil aufblitzt und sachlichkeit als horizont und hintergrund durchgeht.

vienna paint, office development/conversion, vienna
vienna paint, büroausbau/umbau

unit-f, fashion office, vienna, 2000
büro für mode

individuality

in anonymity

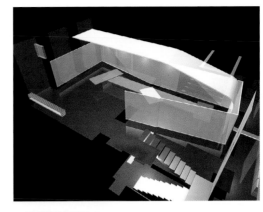

temporary transformation of old spaces; infrastructure behind the membranes
provisorische transformation alter räume; infrastruktur hinter den membranen

individualität

in

surface, space optimized
fläche, raum optimiert

an optimal extent of economic value and spatial diversity has been achieved here within the functional and financial corsets of publicly supported residential building. intelligent measures were applied to dodge restrictions as to technology and building height and to bring about unexpected qualities. the concept given to the twelve apartments is surprisingly three-dimensional – as a stacking of maisonettes. the ones below are directly accessible from the sidewalk, the ones above linked by a street-side access balcony on the third floor, with stockpiled small residential units. opened by half in front, the paned access balcony was able to stretch one meter beyond the permissible height. this served to ingeniously dupe the building regulations that admit only two full-sized stories including a roof structure at an eaves height of 7.5 m. in a similarly simple way, the schematism inherent in cellular framing was resolved by inclining every second divider by half. the maisonettes on the upper floor thus alternately consist of two or three rooms; amounting to five different types of apartments and a rhythmic variation of spatial conditions. the building has a strong opening to the west with well shielded private zones and free spaces. at that point, vertical glass ribbons along the stairways bring much space into the interior and come to generate the volume's optical and practicable transparency with simple details.

im funktionellen und finanziellen korsett staatlich geförderten wohnbaus ist hier ein optimum an nutzwert und raumvielfalt erzielt. vorgegebene technologie und beschränkte bauhöhe sind durch intelligente maßnahmen ausgetrickst und zu unerwarteten qualitäten gebracht. die zwölf wohnungen sind überraschend dreidimensional konzipiert – als stapelung von maisonetten. die unteren sind direkt vom gehsteig zugänglich, die oberen von einem straßenseitigen laubengang im zweiten stock, wo zwischen ihnen noch garçonnieren eingelagert sind. da der verglaste laubengang zur hälfte nach vorne geöffnet wurde, konnte er einen meter über die erlaubte höhe hinausreichen, konnte also die bauvorschrift, die bei 7,5 m traufenhöhe nur zwei vollgeschoße samt dachaufbau zulässt, sinnreich düpiert werden. ebenso simpel ist der immanente schematismus der schottenbauweise aufgelöst, indem jede zweite scheibe zur hälfte schräg gestellt ist. so erhalten die maisonetten auf der oberen etage abwechselnd zwei oder drei zimmer; es gibt damit fünf verschiedene wohnungstypen und eine rhythmische variation der räumlichen verhältnisse. mit gut abgeschirmten privatzonen und freiplätzen ist der bau nach westen stark geöffnet. hier holen die vertikalen glasbänder an den treppen viel raum ins innere und einfache details schaffen die optische und praktikable transparenz des volumens.

court side
hofseite

AFS1, housing
wohnbau

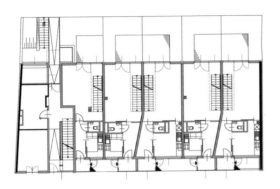

street and court side; ground plan first floor, section; detail
straßen- und hofseite; grundriss erdgeschoß, schnitt; detail

a small villa, excavated and mantled; a basement revaluated into a fully adequate story with new bedrooms and sanitary facilities by means of lowering the level away from the street and sloping the garden on the east side. the most striking measure from the outside is a residential floor extended with a balcony and fliers down to the garden. at first site, the construction appears to be an unspectacular 'low tech', yet it indeed concentrates static, spatial, functional and economic factors to a synthesis that is fully balanced in itself. a horse under the stairway and two slanted columns support the galvanized skeleton of plain steel tubes and sections; the floor and stair treads are made of simple wooden planks, the parapet (as well as the mobile screens in front of the french doors) are of stainless steel grates. parts of the balcony were given a glass floor along the wall to ensure the incidence of light into the basement rooms. the entire garden front thus benefits from an additional layer of usage, a joint and filter between the inside and outside – by means of a construction that adds to the simple massiveness of the old the simple fragility of the new. a structure that also 'glimmers' in itself, between the poles of transparency and screening, sobriety and expressiveness.

quality is ambivalent
qualität ist ambivalent

ausschachtung und überformung einer kleinen villa; aufwertung des sockels zu einem vollwertigen geschoß mit neuen schlaf- und sanitärräumen durch absenken des niveaus von der straße weg und abböschen des gartens an der ostseite. auffälligste maßnahme nach außen ist die erweiterung der wohnetage mit einem balkon samt freitreppe zum garten. die konstruktion erscheint auf den ersten blick als unspektakuläres ‚low tech‘, bündelt aber statische, räumliche, funktionelle und ökonomische faktoren zu einer in sich völlig ausbalancierten synthese. ein bock unter der stiege und zwei schräge stützen tragen das verzinkte gerüst aus einfachen stahlrohren und -profilen; boden und trittstufen sind aus simplen holzbohlen, die brüstung (wie die mobilen screens vor den fenstertüren) mit netzen aus edelstahl. um für die sockelzimmer den lichteinfall zu erhalten, ist der balkon entlang der mauer partiell mit einem glasboden versehen. so erhält die gesamte gartenfront eine zusätzliche nutzschicht als gelenk und filter zwischen drinnen und draußen, und zwar durch eine konstruktion, die der einfachen massivität des alten die einfache fragilität des neuen hinzufügt und die auch in sich selbst ‚flimmert‘ zwischen den polen transparenz und abschirmung, zwischen sachlichkeit und expressivität.

ground plan basement; terrace and balcony facing the garden
grundriss sockelgeschoß; terrasse und balkon zum garten

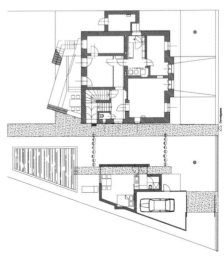

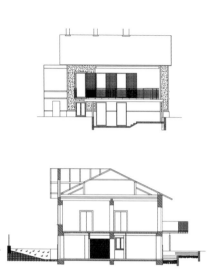

new kitchen; section, views
neue küche; schnitt, ansichten

vogelfrei, screen, k/haus, vienna, 2000
paravent vogelfrei, k/haus

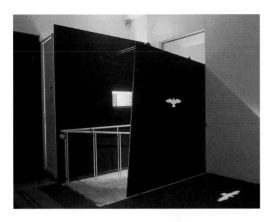

installed exhibit, homage to and critique of transparency
ausstellungsinstallation, hommage und kritik an transparenz

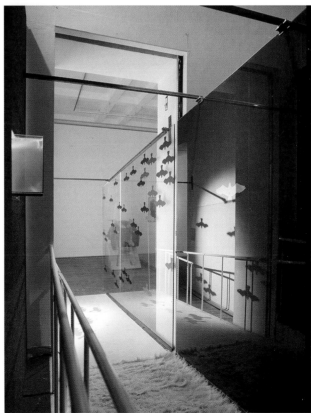

teltow near berlin community center, competition winner, planned
gemeindezentrum, wettbewerbsgewinn, in planung

the winning project at a competition for a new community center on the
outskirts of berlin, close to the former 'death row' in the land of
brandenburg. old listed buildings were given annexes and complex
adaptations. a new solitaire, the new city library was developed on the
site where a garage and a shed had been set up in the old courtyard
ensemble. automobiles are guided under the library building directly
from the street in order to keep the court carfree. the open, slanted
level of the parking ramp is continued in the bottom slab that supports
the new building and folds up above the rear wall toward the roof's
ascending hip. the inclined ceiling above the garage is graded in the
library section, can be furnished with reading spaces in that area, and
also serves as an auditorium for movie performances and readings. the
folded spatial structure extends into the new office wing that complements the principal building oriented to the marketplace; its volume
increases toward the square and joins the court-side unfolding of the
old building's garrets. a specially designed ground zone forms the
access backbone, marks the main entrance on the marketplace, extends
to the information center and the grand staircase in the old building,
to finally continue along the new parish meeting room to the library
entrance hall.

to clinch, at a distance
im clinch, mit distanz

individuality

siegerprojekt des wettbewerbs für ein neues gemeindezentrum am stadtrand von berlin, nahe dem ehemaligen ‚todesstreifen' im land brandenburg. es handelt sich um zubauten und komplexe adaptierungen von
denkmalgeschützten altbauten. wo im alten hofensemble bisher eine
garage und eine scheune standen, entsteht als solitär die neue stadt-
bibliothek. um den hof autofrei zu halten, werden die pkws direkt von
der straße unter das bibliotheksgebäude geleitet. die offene, schiefe
ebene der parkierungsrampe findet ihre fortsetzung in der bodenplatte des
neubaus und faltet sich über die rückwand hinauf zur ansteigenden
dachfläche. die geneigte decke über der garage wird im bibliotheks-
bereich gestuft, kann dort mit leseplätzen möbliert werden und dient
auch als zuschauerbereich für filme und lesungen. die gefaltete raum-
struktur setzt sich fort im neuen bürotrakt. dieser ergänzt den zum
marktplatz orientierten hauptbau; seine kubatur steigt zum platz hin an
und bindet in die hofseitige aufklappung der dachräume des altbaus ein.
eine speziell gestaltete bodenzone bildet das rückgrat der erschließung,
markiert den haupteingang am marktplatz, führt zur bürgerberatung
und zur haupttreppe im altbau und leitet am neuen gemeindesaal im hof
entlang zum entree der bibliothek.

model; section office wing with view of the library
modell; schnitt bürotrakt mit ansicht bibliothek

172

in anonymity

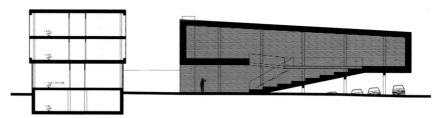

individualität

floors, shelves: interfaces
böden, regale: interfaces

the quarter close to downtown was once marked by small backyard trade and today offers suitable sites for 'creative industries' – of course, to the extent that it survived the redevelopments of the 1970s. the adaptation for an institute of digital imaging first involved a courtyard-sided manufactory, but has since comprised the entire building block. the spaciousness shown by the old halls was not only preserved but intensified into a present-day brisance. ways guided from the court into the building over the ground parts are very much typical of RATAPLAN – a haptic and acoustical sequence of stone, shingle, lattices, concrete, steel and solid timber. industrial parquet replaces the old floors in a 'swimming' fashion, accomplished in terms of esthetic appeal and technical simplicity, on account of irregular walls, set off by stripes of gravel in which easily accessible hot tubes have been installed, and lined by openable wireways' 'metal braids'. shelves of plywood and variable profilit glass, floating in the rooms and equipped with fittings that hail from shipbuilding, are equally incisive: light bodies, light filters, containers and room dividers all in one. felt-covered shelves in the rearmost wing form a new voluminous layer within the old walls. the principle is varied in the sanitary block where new equipment is spun into the old building's niches as a light, technoid 'cocoon'.

das zentrumsnahe viertel war geprägt durch kleingewerbe in hinterhöfen und bietet heute – so es die sanierungen der 1970er jahre überlebte – gute standorte für ‚creative industries‘. die adaptierung für ein institut digitaler bildbearbeitung betraf zuerst ein hofseitiges manufakturgebäude, hat in etappen inzwischen den gesamten baublock erfasst. die großzügigkeit der alten hallen wurde nicht nur bewahrt, sondern durch strukturelle eingriffe in eine heutige brisanz gesteigert. charakteristisch für RATAPLAN ist die führung vom hof ins gebäude über die bodenpartien – eine haptische und akustische sequenz von stein, schotter, gitter, beton, stahl und massivholz bis zum industrieparkett, das in den etagen ‚schwimmend‘ die alten böden ersetzt, von den unregelmäßigen mauern technisch einfach und ästhetisch gelungen durch kiesstreifen abgesetzt, in denen leicht zugänglich die heizungsrohre laufen, und gesäumt mit den öffenbaren ‚metallborten‘ der kabelkanäle. ebenso prägnant die in den räumen ‚schwebenden‘ regale aus sperrholz und variablem profilitglas mit fittings aus dem schiffsbau: lichtkörper, lichtfilter, container und raumteiler in einem. filzbespannte regale bilden im hintersten trakt eine neue raumhältige schicht innerhalb der alten mauern. das prinzip ist im sanitärblock variiert, wo in die nischen des altbaus die neue austattung als leichter, technoider ‚kokon‘ hineingesponnen ist.

in anonymität

entrance hall; court view with glass cube on the second floor

foyer; hofansicht mit glaskubus im 1. stock

vienna paint, office development/conversion and extensions
büro ausbau/umbau und erweiterungen

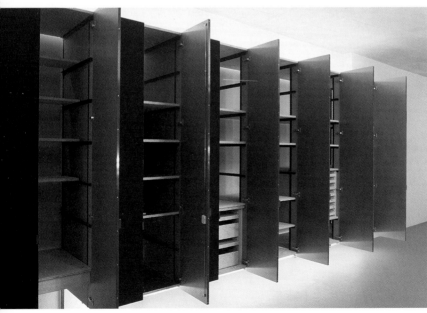

photo studio: wall shelves with black blended felt
fotostudio: wandregale mit schwarz meliertem filz

office loft second floor: shelf elements, screens
büro-loft 1. stock: regalelemente, paravents

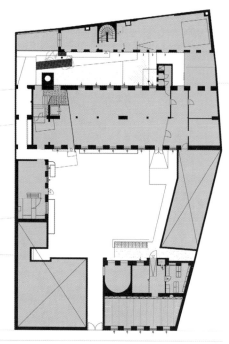

second court; ascent to the office loft; ground plan
zweiter hof; aufgang zum büro-loft; grundriss

RATAPLAN
kohlgasse 11/3, a–1050 wien
tel +43-1-544 06 25, fax +43-1-544 06 25-17
rataplan@rataplan.at, www.rataplan.at

rudi fritz, susanne höhndorf, gerhard huber, martina schöberl, friedel winkler, born between 1957 and 1963; awarded diplomas between 1989 and 1993. studied at vienna tu, berlin tu, stuttgart academy of arts and vienna college of applied arts. guest lecturers at the estonian academy of arts, tallinn. working group since 1989, RATAPLAN since 1993.

buildings, projects (select): literaturhaus, 1989–91; hegergasse residential project (2000 vienna urban renovation prize), 1993–99; vienna paint, office development/conversion and extensions, 1993–2001; kirchengasse residential atelier, 1996; mica music information center austria, 1997; all in vienna. kids' theme park, germany, 1997. passio, stage design, leopoldstadt theater; ARENA, open air site, both 1998; AFS1, housing, 1999; all in vienna. mödling sfd, conversion/annex, 1999–2001; unit-f, fashion office, 2000; vogelfrei, screen, k/haus, 2000; SSG, attic extension, 2001; all in vienna. sfd in niamey, niger, 2001.

planned: ARENA, event center, vienna; 2 residential buildings, vienna 16; kaserngasse, urban villas, vienna; community center, teltow near berlin (competition winner).

rudi fritz, susanne höhndorf, gerhard huber, martina schöberl, friedel winkler, geboren zwischen 1957 und 1963; diplome zwischen 1989 und 1993. studien an der tu wien, tu berlin, kunstakademie stuttgart und hochschule für angewandte kunst wien. gastlehrauftrag an der estonian academy of arts, tallinn. arbeitsgemeinschaft seit 1989, RATAPLAN seit 1993.

bauten, projekte (auswahl): 1989–91 literaturhaus; 1993–99 hegergasse, wohnprojekt (wr. stadterneuerungspreis 2000); 1993–2001 vienna paint, büro ausbau/umbau und erweiterungen; 1996 wohnatelier kirchengasse; 1997 mica music information center austria; alle wien. 1997 kinderfreizeitpark, deutschland. 1998 passio, bühnenbild, theater leopoldstadt; ARENA, open air gelände, wien. 1999 AFS1, wohnbau, wien; 1999–2001 efh mödling, umbau/zubau; 2000 unit-f, büro für mode; 2000 paravent vogelfrei, k/haus wien; 2001 SSG, dachgeschoßausbau, alle wien; 2001 efh in niamey, niger.

in planung: ARENA, veranstaltungszentrum, wien; 2 wohnbauten, wien 16; kaserngasse, stadtvillen, wien; gemeindezentrum, stadt teltow bei berlin (wettbewerbsgewinn).

AFS1, housing / wohnbau, wien
client / bauherr: österreichisches siedlungswerk
collaborators / mitarbeiterInnen: otto arnold, petra gruber, maja lorbek, konrad rautter
statics / statik: josef gebeshuber

vienna paint, office development / conversion and extensions / büro ausbau / umbau und
erweiterungen, wien
client / bauherr: fa. vienna paint
statics / statik: fröhlich und locher, wien

unit-f, fashion office / büro für mode, wien
client / bauherr: unit-f
steelwork / stahlbau: guido wachernig

mödling sfd, conversion/annex / efh mödling, umbau / zubau
client / bauherrn: familie thaller
steelwork / stahlbau: fa. wittmann

vogelfrei, screen / paravent vogelfrei, k-haus wien
curator / kurator: jan tabor
graphic design / grafik: michaela reisinger
steelwork / stahlbau: guido wachernig

community center, competition winner, planned / gemeindezentrum stadt teltow bei berlin,
wettbewerbsgewinn, in planung
client / bauherr: municipality of teltow near berlin / gemeinde teltow
collaborators / mitarbeiterInnen: ingo noack, susanne manthey, robert vörös, martha wolzt
statics / statik: dr. zauft, potsdam

with the kind support of / mit freundlicher unterstützung von:
möbelkunst dietmar bischof, weizbachweg 135, a–8043 graz
fa. KLEINHANS, cad-systeme, heumühlgasse 9, a–1040 wien
vola vertriebs-gmbh, am wasser 4, a–8430 leibnitz
kallco projekt ges.m.b.h., schloßgasse 13, a–1050 wien

KALLCO PROJEKT™

architekturzentrum wien; springer-verlag wien new york; text: © otto kapfinger
photo credits: © by the architects and: otto arnold: 163; markus tomaselli: 157, 159, 161–163, 165–167;
169–171, 173, 175–178

riccione

While going through their novitiates at local studios, Bortolotti, Ramoni, Cede & co. made use of the arts context to formulate substantial, para-architectonic statements in public urban spaces. Kitzbühel, for example, attempted in 1996 to garnish the 'dead season' between the peaks with cultural events for the residents themselves. For three weeks, riccione draped the façade of a dilapidated old building with a net designating the exile status given to the contemporariness of building culture within a thoroughly commercialized society of tourism. riccione marked that net with a poem by American poet Emily Dickinson, 'I dwell in possibility, a fairer house than prose…' The position held by the non-adjusted, the outsider's vision in a dull environment emerging from these lines is neither melancholic nor pathetic, but rather cheerful, uninhibited, and supported by sober optimism. riccione as a group stand for their generation's mentality that is attached to a smiling, not a grim guerrilla war. Seeking loopholes for progressive, intelligent ideas in the niches of an ignorant reality – which still marks the building climate in the Alps' furrows regardless of much current progress – they have come to realize: to dwell in possibility … riccione belong to the hard core of the young 'Architekturforum Tirol'. Thanks to their initiative, and that of MA'nGO, Astrid Tschapeller and Michael Steinlechner, a working meeting developed in 1999 to gather thirty young architects and groups from

To Dwell in Possibility
Daheim im Vorstellbaren

Als Bortolotti, Ramoni, Cede & Co. noch in lokalen Büros ihre Praxis-jahre abarbeiteten, nützten sie den Kunstkontext für beachtliche, para-architektonische Statements in öffentlichen Stadträumen. Als etwa Kitzbühel 1996 versuchte, die ‚tote' Zeit zwischen den Hochsaisonen mit Kulturereignissen für die Einwohner selbst zu garnieren, bekleideten riccione für drei Wochen die Fassade eines baufälligen Altbaus mit einem Netz, das den Exil-Status jeder baukulturellen Zeitgenossenschaft innerhalb der durchkommerzialisierten Tourismusgesellschaft benannte. riccione schrieben auf dieses Netz ein Poem der amerikanischen Lyrikerin Emily Dickinson: ‚I dwell in possibility, a fairer house than prose…' Die Position des Unangepassten, die Vision des Außenseiters in dumpfer Umgebung ist in diesen Zeilen weder melancholisch noch pathetisch ausgesprochen, sondern heiter, unverkrampft, mit nüchternem Optimismus. riccione als Gruppe stehen für eine solche Mentalität des lächelnden, nicht des verbissenen Partisanenkampfs ihrer Generation, die in den Nischen der ignoranten Wirklichkeit – welche in den Alpen-furchen trotz vieler aktueller Fortschritte nach wie vor das Bauklima prägt – Schlupfwege für progressive, intelligente Ideen sucht und findet: to dwell in possibility… riccione zählen zum harten Kern im jungen Architekturforum Tirol. Durch ihre Initiative entstand zusammen mit MA'nGO, Astrid Tschapeller und Michael Steinlechner 1999 ein

School Extension, Zirl
Schulerweiterung

Austria and Germany in Italy's Briolo – a follow-up seminar is currently being organized. Between 1997 and 2000, they were among the prize-winners at eight different competitions, and were awarded first prize three times. Their architecture – even in highly urban designs – show an ease and an attitude that is strongly differentiated for the respective context: Agility in terms of a loose simplicity of solutions rather than in a literal or constructive sense. Material, construction, form etc. are never tapered in a strained fashion, they are brought to such a point that the equilibrium between these factors and others casually reaches a con-clusive atmosphere – difficult to describe but immediately perceptible. A becoming apparent in buildings of the piece of accomplished life to which architecture is meant to offer a stage. 'Riccione is the Innsbruckers' Iésolo,' wrote Patricia Grzonka, 'the Tirolians' weekend longing.' An Adriatic seaside resort serving as a program for architecture? An indi-cation, at any rate, of a critical vital involvement that is void of dogma and argues for an everyday sensual dimension in building and living acquired without opulence.

Arbeitstreffen von dreißig jungen ArchitektInnen und Gruppen aus Österreich und Deutschland im italienischen Briol – ein zweites Seminar dieser Art ist in Vorbereitung. Zwischen 1997 und 2000 kamen sie bei acht Wettbewerben in die Preisränge, davon dreimal an die erste Stelle. Ihre Architektur – auch bei hochurbanen Entwürfen – zeigt eine Leichtigkeit und eine jeweils für den Kontext stark differenzierte Haltung: Leichtigkeit weniger im wörtlichen oder konstruktiven Sinn als in der lockeren Einfachheit der Problemlösung. Material, Konstruktion, Form etc. sind niemals überanstrengt zugespitzt, sind jeweils so weit getrieben, bis die Balance dieser und anderer Faktoren zwanglos eine stimmige Atmosphäre erreicht – schwer beschreibbar, aber unvermittelt spürbar. Ein Vorschein im Baulichen auf das Stück gelungenen Lebens, dem Architektur doch die Bühne geben sollte. ‚Riccione‘, schrieb Patricia Grzonka, ‚ist das Jesolo der Innsbrucker, die Wochenendsehn-sucht der Tiroler‘. Ein adriatischer Badeort als Architekturprogramm? Ein Hinweis jedenfalls auf kritisches, lebensbejahendes Engagement ohne Dogmatik, für eine alltägliche, sinnliche Dimension im Bauen und Leben, die auch ohne Opulenz erreichbar ist.

K. Office and House, Reith near Seefeld, 1998-2000
Büro und Haus K., Reith bei Seefeld

Urban History Deconstructed
Stadtgeschichte dekonstruiert

Following the 'anschluss' in 1938, the Tiroler Landhaus in the center of Innsbruck was given a new south wing, the 'Gauhaus'. Right across, a monument, the 'Franzosendenkmal', was set up in 1948 in memory of the liberation from Nazi dictatorship. This gateway reflects the building's five-axis central projection, both structurally and proportionally, in an irritating way never discussed before in that town. On the square in between, riccione then projected the outlines of a Nazi labor camp that once existed on the eastern outskirts of Innsbruck. The film broadcast in a room of the Gallery in the Taxispalais revealed the paradox, latent in that urban space, to become manifest in the critical space of art.

Das Tiroler Landhaus im Zentrum von Innsbruck erhielt 1938 nach dem ,Anschluss' einen neuen Südtrakt, das ,Gauhaus'. Direkt gegenüber entstand 1948 das ,Franzosendenkmal' als Monument der Befreiung von der Nazi-Diktatur. Auf irritierende, in der Stadt niemals diskutierte Weise spiegelt dieser Torbau strukturell und in den Proportionen den fünfachsigen Mittelrisalit des Nazi-Gebäudes. riccione projizierten nun auf den Platz dazwischen die Umrisse eines NS-Arbeitslagers, das an der östlichen Peripherie von Innsbruck existierte. Die Filmübertragung in einen Raum der Taxisgalerie machte das im Stadtraum latente Paradox im kritischen Kunstraum manifest.

in possibility

to dwell

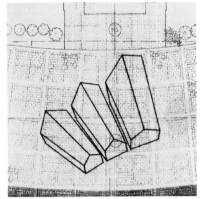

Video stills; square with monument; draft
Video-Stills; Platz mit Denkmal; Entwurf

The house – inhabited by the clients who run a long-standing publishing company for postcards and photographs – was given an annex to accommodate an office, bookstock, postcard shop, and garage. Full use was made of the legally permissible volume in this narrow environment, where agriculture and the villa milieu flow into one another in small dimensions, and the enlargement was set into the garden like a fine mobile pavilion. On account of the photosensitive photographs, prints and cards, special attention was to be paid to the kind of lighting and protection against the sun. The window bands show alternating, fixed UV glazings with exterior awnings and unfoldable larchen elements for ventilation purposes. The garage and office are set over one another as reinforced-concrete tables. Colored, fibrated cement slabs cover the wooden lightweight façades. A light slit serving the garage lifts the 'caravan' above the lawn level, and a roof terrace is attached to the old building.

A Caravaning Publishing House
Verlagsbüro im Caravan

to dwell

Das Haus, in dem die Bauherren wohnen und einen traditionsreichen Postkarten- und Fotoverlag führen, erhielt einen Zubau für Büro, Lager, Postkartenshop und Garage. In der engen Umgebung, wo Landwirtschaft und Villenmilieu kleinräumig ineinanderfließen, wurde der Anbau bei voller Ausnutzung des rechtlich möglichen Volumens wie ein feiner, mobiler Pavillon in den Garten gesetzt. Wegen der lichtempfindlichen Fotografien, Drucke und Karten musste auf die Art der Belichtung und den Sonnenschutz besonderes Augenmerk gelegt werden. Die Fensterbänder zeigen alternierend fixe UV-Verglasung mit äußeren Markisen und zur Belüftung aufklappbare Elemente aus Lärchenholz. Garage und Büro sind als Stahlbetontische übereinandergestellt. Die Holz-Leichtbaufassaden haben eine Deckschicht aus gefärbten Faserzementplatten; ein Lichtschlitz für die Garage hebt den ‚Caravan' über das Rasenniveau; Dachterrasse im Anschluss an den Altbau.

West side, section; eastern view
Westseite, Schnitt; Ostansicht

in possibility

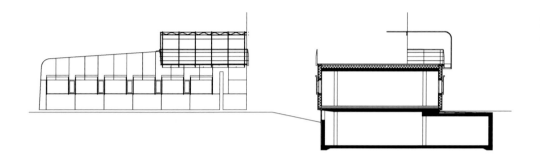

Defner Office Building and Publishing House
Büro- und Verlagshaus Defner

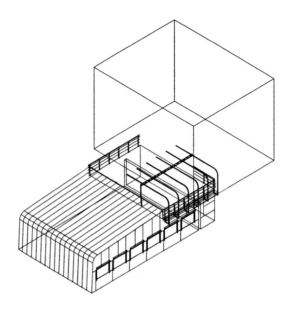

West side with view into the garage; axonometry
Westseite mit Einblick zur Garage; Axonometrie

School Extension, Zirl, Tirol, 1999–2001
Schulerweiterung

to dwell in possibility

daheim

Scheerbart's Dream of Space
Scheerbarts Raumtraum

To the south of the old secondary school, a new two-story building was set up on the declining plot such that the entire area was given a new identity with little-visible volumes and simple means. The gym sunk into the terrain represents the extension's new center, around which all ways and floor spaces are organized and are separated merely by layers of panings. An accessway runs through the newly created courtyard at the upper level from which a panorama develops to cover the interplay between the inner courtyard, open upwards to the southern sun, and the annexed interior space oriented 'downwards' to northern and eastern lights. Flooded from all sides with brightness, the hall and the fresh concept of color and artificial light welcome those incoming with an ambiance of cheerful openness. Filtered by one or – depending on the perspective – several layers of glass, the peripheral colors of corridor walls, doors and floors show teasing shades. 'What's called for is not more light, but more colorful light, 'Scheerbart's maxim, is simply and effectively applied here to generate a kaleidoscopic luminous atmosphere. Functionally and spatially, the school for special education at the upper level and the polytechnical school at the lower level together form a wreath that reflects the exteriorly fastened courtyard topic into the interior via the gym.

Südlich der alten Hauptschule ist ein zweigeschoßiger Neubau so ins abfallende Gelände gesetzt, dass mit wenig sichtbarer Kubatur und mit einfachen Mitteln eine neue Identität der gesamten Anlage erzielt wird. Die ins Terrain gesenkte Turnhalle bildet das Zentrum der Erweiterung. Um sie herum und nur getrennt durch Schichten von Verglasungen sind alle Wege und Nutzflächen organisiert. Der Zugang erfolgt von dem neu geschaffenen Hof auf der oberen Ebene und von dort erschließt sich auch der Überblick über das Wechselspiel zwischen dem zur Südsonne und nach oben offenen Innenhof mit dem zum Nord- und Ostlicht orientierten und 'nach unten' offenen Binnenraum des Zubaus. Die von allen Seiten lichtdurchflutete Halle und das frische Farb- und Kunstlichtkonzept empfangen mit einer Atmosphäre heiterer Offenheit. Durch eine oder – je nach Standpunkt – mehrere Glasschichten gefiltert, vexieren die peripheren Farbtöne von Flurwänden, Türen und Böden in den verschiedensten Nuancen. Scheerbarts Maxime – 'nicht mehr Licht, mehr Farblicht muss es heißen' – ist hier simpel und effektiv für eine kaleidoskopische Lichtstimmung angewendet. Funktionell und räumlich bilden die Sonderschule auf der oberen und der Polytechnische Lehrgang auf der unteren Ebene einen Kranz, der das außen angeschlagene Hofthema über die Turnhalle ins Innere spiegelt.

Gym; section, connection with old building
Turnhalle; Schnitt, Anschluss zum Altbau

im vorstellbaren

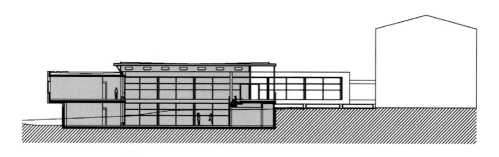

Lobby and hall; court between the extension and existing structures
Foyer und Hallenraum; Hof zwischen Erweiterung und Bestand

Building Along the River
Bauen am Fluss

As a factor generating urban space, residential building has not yielded much over the past decades. The small structure in the center of Innsbruck at least indicates an approach to how new typologies may evolve in spite of tight budgets and clients' fear of innovation. The building replaces an obsolete business house, densified in a central location showing mixed occupancies – shops and offices on the ground floor –, and avails of a view out to the river and the mountains. At once, it creates a fresh sense of permeability between the river space and the adjacent urban body, and provides a universally modulated structural sculpture as an alternative to the common drawers profile. The objective was to give every apartment a two-sided orientation regardless of their central-corridor accessibility, i.e. to enjoy the view to the river and the Nordkette mountains, as well as the south side. A paned elevator and open stairways lend the slit inserted between the separate wings an optimal quality of transparency, supported by a broadly paned ground floor that is set off from the embankment walk. The concrete structure projects far out towards the River Inn, sets free the corners roundabout, shows cross-story elements and varied balcony positions. Floor-to-floor French doors and windows form spacious filters between the inside and outside, while stretching the entire scale in spite of minimized heights.

Als Faktor urbaner Raumbildung hat der Wohnbau in den letzten Jahrzehnten wenig vorzuweisen. Der kleine Bau im Zentrum von Innsbruck zeigt immerhin Ansätze, wie trotz enger Budgets und Innovationsangst der Bauträger neue Typologien entstehen könnten. Der Bau ersetzt ein veraltetes Geschäftshaus, verdichtet in zentraler Lage mit gemischter Nutzung – Läden und Büros im Erdgeschoß –, nimmt den Ausblick zum Fluss und zu den Bergen wahr, schafft zugleich eine neue Durchlässigkeit zwischen Flussraum und dem anschließenden Stadtkörper und bietet statt des üblichen Schubladkastenprofils eine allseitig modulierte Bauplastik mit dem Anspruch, trotz Mittelgangerschließung jede Wohnung nach zwei Seiten zu orientieren, d.h. sowohl am Blick auf den Fluss und die Nordkette als auch an der Südseite partizipieren zu lassen. Verglaster Lift und offene Treppe bringen dem Schlitz zwischen den separierten Trakten optimale Transparenz, unterstützt durch das breit verglaste, von der Uferpromenade zurückgesetzte Erdgeschoß. Die Betonstruktur kragt weit zum Inn hin aus, stellt die Ecken rundum frei, hat geschoßübergreifende Elemente und variierte Balkonpositionen. Raumhohe Fenstertüren bzw. französische Fenster bilden großzügige Filter zwischen Innen und Außen, strecken trotz minimierter Höhen den Maßstab des Ganzen.

Concrete structure carcass
Rohbau Betonstruktur

Herzog Siegmund Ufer Residential and Office Building
Wohn- und Bürohaus Herzog Siegmund Ufer

Section; northern view with River Inn
Schnitt; Nordansicht mit Innfluss

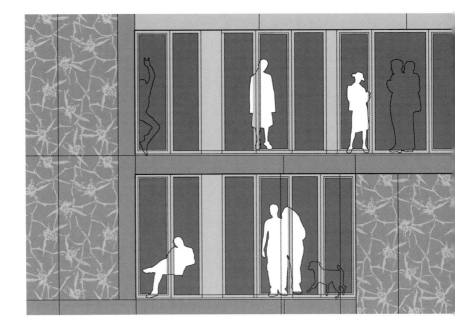

Façade detail; northern view, western view
Fassadendetail; Nordansicht, Westansicht

Tivoli Neu Ice and Event Stadiums, competition, 2nd prize, Innsbruck, 2001
Eis- und Veranstaltungshallen Tivoli Neu, Wettbewerb, 2. Preis

Second prize at the EU-level competition for a conversion of the 1964 Olympic Ice Stadium to put up variable occupancies and for a new smaller ice stadium with catering and administrative facilities. The old hall's formerly planked roof structure with obliquely projecting soffits was exposed and made visible within and without, and the northern and southern fronts were reglazed. The marked old silhouette was thus transformed into a novel, constructive spatial profile. The topic of a 'floating' table was continued in terms of a double fold above the new low hall and the five-story street wing: a powerful, horizontally mounted signet of functions in front of the valley side precipices, referring clearly to the soccer stadium within sight. A new basement along the street side accommodates the joint lobby and a large terrace on the second floor with a restaurant and access to the bleachers' main level.

Urban Profile
Starkes Stadtprofil

Zweiter Preis des EU-weiten Wettbewerbs zum Umbau des Olympia-Eisstadions von 1964 für variable Nutzungen und zum Neubau einer kleineren Eishalle mit ergänzender Gastronomie und Administration. Die vorher verkleidete Dachkonstruktion der alten Halle mit den schräg auskragenden Untersichten wird freigelegt und innen wie außen sichtbar gemacht, Nord- und Südfront werden neu verglast. So wird die markante alte Silhouette in ein neues, konstruktives Raumprofil transformiert. Das Thema des ‚schwebenden' Tisches wird als zweifache Abkantung über die neue, niedrige Halle und den fünfstöckigen Straßentrakt weitergezogen: ein starkes, horizontal gelagertes Signet der Funktionen vor den Steilhängen der Talflanken mit klarem Bezug zu dem in Sichtweite befindlichen Fußballstadion. Ein neuer Sockel an der Straßenseite enthält das gemeinsame Foyer und eine große Terrasse im ersten Stock mit Restaurant und Zutritt zur Hauptebene der Tribünen.

Functional and spatial arrangement; southern view
Funktionelle und räumliche Gliederung; Südansicht

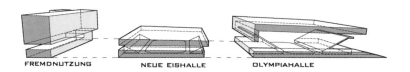

FREMDNUTZUNG   NEUE EISHALLE   OLYMPIAHALLE

im vorstellbaren

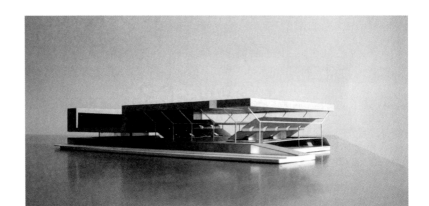

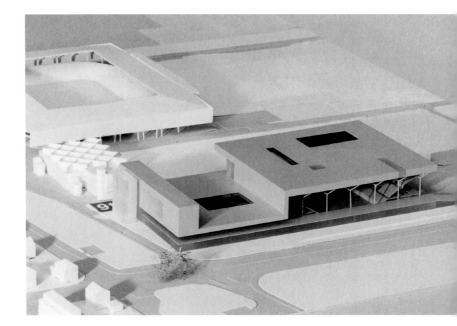

View of model; northern view
Modelldarstellung; Nordansicht

Innsbruck Alpinists Museum, extension, experts selection procedure, 1st prize, 2001
Alpenvereinsmuseum Innsbruck, Erweiterung, Gutachterverfahren, 1. Preis

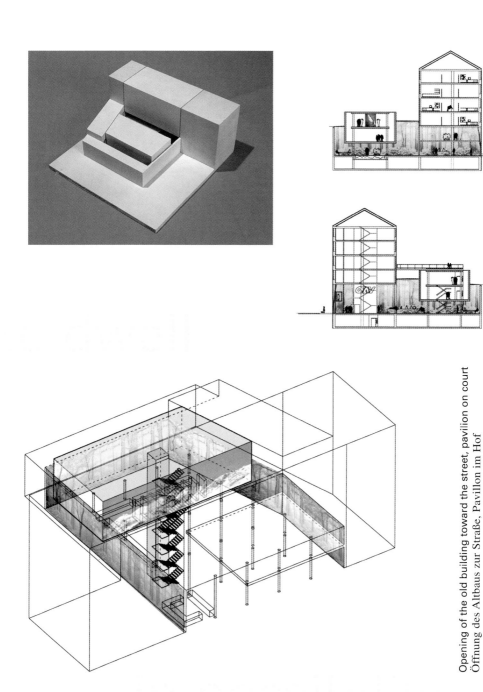

Opening of the old building toward the street, pavilion on court
Öffnung des Altbaus zur Straße, Pavillon im Hof

riccione
Mariahilfstraße 22, A–6020 Innsbruck
Tel +43-512-278 590, Fax +43-512-278 590-49
riccione@aon.at

Clemens Bortolotti, born in Innsbruck in 1967; studied architecture at Innsbruck TU; awarded diploma in 1995. Assistant at the Department of Building Construction, Prof. Giencke, Innsbruck TU, 1995–2000.
Tilwin Cede, born in Innsbruck in 1965; studied architecture at Innsbruck TU; awarded diploma in 1995. Assistant at the Department of City Planning, Prof. Langhof, Innsbruck TU, 1995–2000.
Mario Ramoni, born in Salzburg in 1961; studied architecture at Innsbruck TU; awarded diploma in 1992. Lecturer with Prof. Giencke, 1997–98; assistant with Prof. Langhof, 1998–99, both Innsbruck TU.
Buildings, projects (select): Defner Office Building and Publishing House, Innsbruck-Igls, 1997–98; Innsbruck-Igls Row Houses (together with A. Fessler), 1998–99; Office and Residential Building, Reith near Seefeld, Tirol, 1999–2000 (together with Wolfgang Ohnmacht); Technikerstraße Residential and Office Building, Innsbruck, competition, 1st prize (together with Helmut Reitter and Michael Pfleger), 2000; 'Housing 2000 – Villages/ Places in Town' workshop, Bonn, 2000. Planned / under construction: Mimm House, Innsbruck, 2001–02. Exhibitions: Architekturforum Tirol, color installation, 1996; Installation on the Tiroler Landhausplatz (on the occasion of the 'Continuous Towns – Urban Situations' exhibition), Gallery in the Taxispalais, Innsbruck, 2000.

Clemens Bortolotti, geboren 1967 in Innsbruck; Architekturstudium an der TU Innsbruck; 1995 Diplom. 1995–2000 Assistent am Institut für Hochbau, Prof. Giencke, TU Innsbruck.
Tilwin Cede, geboren 1965 in Innsbruck; Architekturstudium an der TU Innsbruck; 1995 Diplom. 1995–2000 Assistent am Institut für Städtebau, Prof. Langhof, TU Innsbruck.
Mario Ramoni, geboren 1961 in Salzburg; Architekturstudium an der TU Innsbruck; 1992 Diplom. 1997–98 Lehrauftrag am Institut für Hochbau, Prof. Giencke, TU Innsbruck. 1998–99 Assistent am Institut für Städtebau, Prof. Langhof, TU Innsbruck.
Bauten, Projekte (Auswahl): 1997–98 Büro- und Verlagshaus Defner, Innsbruck-Igls; 1998–99 Reihenhäuser Innsbruck-Igls (mit A. Fessler); 1999–2000 Büro- und Wohnhaus Reith bei Seefeld, Tirol (mit Wolfgang Ohnmacht); 2000 Wohn- und Bürohaus Technikerstraße, Innsbruck (Wettbewerb, 1. Preis, mit Helmut Reitter und Michael Pfleger); Workshop ‚Wohnen 2000 – Orte in der Stadt', Bonn. In Planung und Bau: 2001–02 Haus Mimm, Innsbruck. Ausstellungen: 1996 Architekturforum Tirol, Farb-Installation; 2000 Installation am Tiroler Landhausplatz (im Rahmen der Ausstellung ‚Die andauernden Städte – Urbane Situationen'), Galerie im Taxispalais, Innsbruck.

College of Special Education, Polytechnical and Secondary Schools, extensions / Schul-
erweiterung Sonderpädagogische Schule, Polytechnischer Lehrgang und Hauptschule, Zirl
Client / Bauherr: Municipality / Gemeinde Zirl
Collaborator / Mitarbeiter: Rudolf Palme
Statics / Statik: Alfred Brunnsteiner

Office and Residential Building / Büro- und Wohnhaus, Reith bei Seefeld in Tirol
Client / Bauherr: Helmut and/und Margit Köll
Statics / Statik: Wolfgang Philipp

Installation on the Tiroler Landhausplatz / Installation am Tiroler Landhausplatz (im Rahmen
der Ausstellung 'Die andauernden Städte – Urbane Situationen'), Galerie im Taxispalais,
Innsbruck
Client / Bauherr: Galerie im Taxispalais

Defner Office Building and Publishing House / Büro- und Verlagshaus Defner, Innsbruck-Igls
Clients / Bauherr: Thomas and/und Gerlinde Defner
Statics / Statik: Armin Weber

Herzog Siegmund Ufer Residential and Office Building / Wohn- und Bürohaus Herzog
Siegmund Ufer, Innsbruck
Client / Bauherr: Renova / Innerebner – Bauträger
Collaborator / Mitarbeiter: Christopher Perktold
Statics / Statik: Friedrich Oberauer

Tivoli Neu Ice and Event Stadiums, EU level, open 1-stage competition, 2nd prize / Eis- und
Veranstaltungshallen Tivoli Neu, EU-weiter, offener, 1-stufiger Wettbewerb, 2. Preis, Innsbruck
Client / Bauherr: Innsbrucker Sportanlagen Errichtungs- und Verwertungs GmbH (ISPA)
Statics / Statik: Christian Zoidl

Innsbruck Alpinists Museum, extension, experts selection procedure, 1st prize /
Alpenvereinsmuseum Innsbruck, Erweiterung, Gutachterverfahren, 1. Preis
Client / Bauherr: Österreichischer Alpenverein

With the kind support of / Mit freundlicher Unterstützung von:
Innerebner Bau GmbH, Rennweg 30, A–6020 Innsbruck

Kultur

Architekturzentrum Wien; Springer-Verlag Wien New York; Text: © Otto Kapfinger
Photo credits: © by the architects and: Die Fotografen: 201; Robert Fleischanderl: 187; Martin Tusch:
183, 185, 189–191, 193, 195; Günter Wett: 194

franz sam

although he has been roaming through the scene in and around vienna for some years, sam is hardly known for his own work. he supervised some spectacular things, especially in terms of constructive conversions, as a project leader with coop himmelb(l)au – the falkestraße roof completion, the seibersdorf research center, the ufa movie center in dresden. the stridency taken by the approach, more so than the expressive gesture of the viennese deconstructivist pioneers, continued to be present in his independent constructions as of the mid-1990s. sam prefers to design and review his projects with a four-color pen. with calligraphically jotted diagrams, he brings out the essentials of principles, lines of force, joints and spatial cross-sections – like black, red, blue bowshots in the white space of paper. the feeling for bearing and loading is perceived in every crossing, every superimposition of colors, in which the focusing, tensions and outflow of forces is anticipated. his extraordinary, ingenious talent was already noticed in building school. the pleasure he takes in the complexity of constructional statics has visibly developed from the abstract mathematical level on to sensual-projective space. each of his strokes is concrete and abbreviates the simultaneity of technical and creative vision. lines' conciseness originates in the sharpness of looks. this is an x-ray look that sounds the old stonework, complex vault formations, the patchwork of reinforced

radicality as continuity
radikalität als kontinuität

er ist schon einige jahre in der szene in und um wien unterwegs, mit den eigenen arbeiten aber bisher kaum bekannt. zehn jahre lang hat er als projektleiter bei coop himmelb(l)au einige spektakuläre dinge vor allem in der konstruktiven umsetzung betreut – den dachausbau falke-straße, das forschungszentrum seibersdorf, das ufa-kinozentrum in dresden. in seinen selbständigen bauten ab mitte der 1990er jahre ist primär die schärfe des ansatzes, weniger der expressive gestus der wiener dekonstruktivisten-pioniere weiter präsent. sam entwirft und bespricht seine projekte am liebsten mit dem vierfarbenstift. mit kalli-grafisch hingeschriebenen diagrammen bringt er prinzipien, kraftlinien, gelenke und raumquerschnitte eines projekts auf den punkt. seine linien sind federnd – wie schwarze, rote, blaue pfeilschüsse im weißen raum des papiers. in jeder kreuzung, jeder überlagerung der farben schwingt das gefühl für tragen und lasten mit, antizipiert sich das bündeln, spannen und abfließen von kräften. schon in der baufachschule war sein ungewöhnliches ingeniöses talent aufgefallen. seine freude an der komplexität von baustatik hat sich von der abstrakten, mathe-matischen ebene sichtlich in den sinnlich-projektiven raum weiterent-wickelt. jeder seiner striche ist konkret, ein kürzel für die simultaneität von technischer und gestalterischer vision. die prägnanz des strichs hat ihren ursprung in der schärfe des blicks. es ist ein röntgenblick,

stelzer office building on company premises
bürogebäude stelzer im firmenareal

concrete structures or terrains for their courses of forces, their temporal and material stratifications, benchmarks and weak points; no data check in art history, but an analytical visualization of static findings and sedimented architectural histories. sam exercised this look in his youth as a hobby geologist while hunting through the highly fossiliferous loess landscape on the banks of the danube and traisen and later as a trainee taking part in archeological excavations in the mid east. his first projects in the krems area are all implants into historical substance. the radicality of his interventions does not follow the pubescent cliché of overcoming the past or a shallow dissociation from history. rather, his crystal-clear interventions are developed with a knowledgeable respect for the permanence of historical facts. the sensitive practical examination of given circumstances is followed by his unaffected reaction, the highly concentrated opening and overlaying of the old – often fiendishly tricky in statical and spatial terms – with today's sovereignly mastered technology and new spatial demands.

der altes mauerwerk, komplexe gewölbe-formationen, flickwerk von stahlbetonstrukturen oder geländeformen auf ihre spannungsverläufe abtastet, auf ihre zeitlichen und materiellen schichtungen, auf fest- und schwachpunkte durchleuchtet; kein kunsthistorischer datencheck, sondern analytisches vergegenwärtigen statischer befunde und sedimentierter baugeschichten. sam hat diesen blick in der jugend als hobby-geologe beim durchstöbern der fossilreichen lösslandschaft an donau- und traisenufer geübt und später als praktikant bei archäologischen grabungen im nahen osten perfektioniert. seine ersten arbeiten im raum von krems sind durchwegs implantate in historische bausubstanz. die radikalität seiner eingriffe folgt nicht dem pubertären klischee einer überwindung oder platten distanzierung von geschichte. seine glas-klaren interventionen sind vielmehr mit wissendem respekt vor der permanenz historischer fakten entwickelt. dem sensiblen, praktischen sehen dieser gegebenheiten folgt seine ungekünstelte reaktion, das hochkonzentrierte öffnen und überlagern des alten – des statisch und räumlich oft teuflisch vertrackten – mit der souverän beherrschten technik und den neuen raumansprüchen der gegenwart.

sacha/katzensteiner law office, conversion, krems/donau, 2001
anwaltskanzlei sacha/katzensteiner, umbau

as

radicality

the builder's cockpit
cockpit des baumeisters

the company has long maintained a warehouse for building material and barracks for its work force in a macadam pit close to a railroad station. the master builder himself is an architect, has a lot to do in the rural vicinity, but sees little demands for architecture. he fetched sam to design a new building for his company's headquarters. executed by his own masons, a manifesto of the possible thus developed on the small town's outskirts above an arsenal of customariness. one upon another, sam stacked up three zones: staff rooms / an archive form a compact basement in the embankment; spatial cantilever beams, the offices above radiate from the street level far out into the area's 'pit' and also roof the basement zone forecourt. at right angles, a cockpit studio was added to the offices, propped open to the west, as a conclusion and reference to the company's logo. the three zones are sharply differentiated by means of construction, material and light lanes, but at once intensively linked by vertically overlapping spaces of motion and 'interior windows'. all building components are thoroughly worked through in static/plastic terms, tuned up to their essence in terms of weight savings and optical lightness (concrete covers' eroded tension zones). this optimization is also articulated in shape, such as in six different concrete columns and their subtle dance below the main level that is conceived as a continuous beam.

in einer schottergrube neben dem bahnhof hat die firma seit langem ihr baustofflager und baracken für die belegschaft. der baumeister ist auch architekt, hat in der ländlichen umgebung viel zu tun, doch besteht wenig nachfrage nach architektur. für den neubau des firmensitzes holte er sam als entwerfer. ausgeführt von den eigenen bauleuten, entstand so an der peripherie der kleinstadt über dem arsenal des alltäglichen ein manifest des möglichen. sam stapelte drei zonen übereinander: belegschaftsräume /archiv bilden den kompakten sockel in der böschung; die büros darüber strahlen vom straßenniveau als räumliche kragbalken weit in die ‚grube' des geländes hinaus, überdachen auch den vorplatz der sockelzone; quer zu den nach westen aufgespreizten büros ist als abschluss und referenz an das firmenlogo das cockpit-studio aufgesetzt. die drei zonen sind durch konstruktion, material und lichtschneisen scharf differenziert, zugleich durch vertikal übergreifende bewegungsräume und ‚innere fenster' intensiv verbunden. sämtliche bauteile sind statisch/plastisch durchgearbeitet, für gewichtsersparnis und optische leichtigkeit auf ihre essenz getrimmt (ausgehöhlte zugzonen der betondecken u.a.), und diese optimierung ist auch gestalthaft zur sprache gebracht, wie etwa im subtilen tanz der sechs verschiedenen beton-stützen unter der als durchlaufträger konzipierten hauptebene.

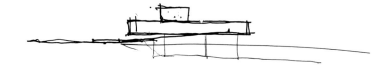

views from storage yard, lower level
ansichten vom lagerplatz, untere ebene

stelzer office building
bürogebäude stelzer

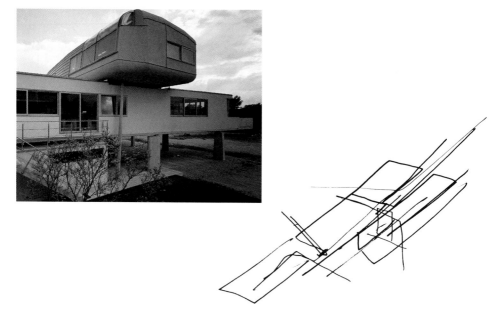

views from the street, square; concept draft
ansichten von der straße, vorplatz; konzeptskizze

stelzer office building
bürogebäude stelzer

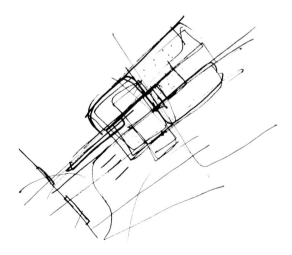

concept draft; in the cockpit
konzeptskizze; im cockpit

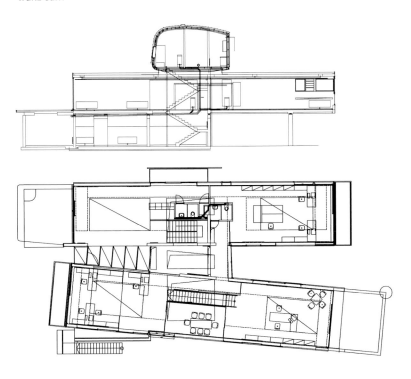

entrance hall; ground plan office level, section
foyer; grundriss büroebene, schnitt

a vault in the city's medieval center was sent through a time machine to and fro: shifted into reverse, the character originally given to the barrel-vaulted rooms reappeared; shifted into forward gear, there came into view the former mint, the bicycle shop fit in subsequently, and finally the nonfunctional location turned into the most modern bar in the vicinity of vienna. sam's interventions blend a radical 'revelation' that gets down to the root of a given substance with a partial 'velation' of space, creating the new function openly and ephemerally. after removing all internal fittings, the relatively recent plastering was knocked off the vault. in some sections, the medieval skin emerged from underneath with impressions of the formwork. these original wall parts were preserved and lined with steel edges. the other surfaces were either covered with whitewash or steel sheets to hang up posters, or with modern osb shuttering panels that also serve as bottom plates and tabletops. the new plasterwork is colored in red, an 'atmospheric plaster' set above several sitting and standing areas. the entire furnishing of metal, glass, sheet metal and panels reflects the bearing associated with the act of laconically skinning off the unessential and precise paperings of locations with the today's minimalist layer.

the layer of today
die schicht der gegenwart

ein gewölbe im mittelalterlichen stadtkern wurde nach beiden seiten durch die zeitmaschine geschickt: im rückwärtsgang kam der ursprüngliche charakter der tonnengewölbten räume wieder zum vorschein; im vorwärtsgang wurde aus der ehemaligen münzstätte, dem später eingebauten fahrradladen und dem zuletzt funktionslosen ort die modernste bar im umkreis wiens. sams eingriffe verschmelzen die radikale, an die wurzel der vorgefundenen substanz gehende ‚enthüllung' mit einer partiellen, die neue funktion offen und ephemer herstellenden ‚verhüllung' des raumes. nach dem entfernen aller einbauten wurde auch der relativ junge verputz vom gewölbe abgeschlagen. darunter zeigte sich in einigen abschnitten die mittelalterliche haut mit den abdrücken der gewölbeschalung. diese originalen wandteile wurden konserviert und mit stahlkanten gesäumt. die übrigen flächen wurden entweder mit weißem putz überzogen, mit blechplatten zur affichierung von postern oder mit modernen osb-schalungsplatten bekleidet, die auch als boden- und tischplatten dienen. über einigen sitz- und stehbereichen ist der neuputz als ‚stimmungspflaster' rot gefärbt. die gesamte möblierung aus metall, glas, blech und platten spiegelt die haltung des lakonischen enthäutens vom unwesentlichen und des präzisen ausschlagens des ortes mit der minimalistischen schicht der gegenwart.

view from the entrance; floor, panels, furniture – one material
blick vom eingang; boden, paneele, möbel materialident

radikalität

hendrik bar
bar hendrik

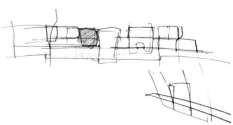

windscreen; façade; concept draft
windfang; fassade; konzeptskizze

bar furniture; concept drafts
barmöbel; konzeptskizzen

the starting point was a dilapidated investors' project, a rural barn. the unambitious volume along one of the city's main access roads was unacceptable to wolfgang krejs, the local building director, who called for a change and to consult an architect. sam's elbowroom was minimal as to economy and space, 'i could barely deviate by 8 cm from the cross-section with a saddle roof. my intention was very simple: i first pressed down on the north-side roofage. this deformed the entire structure. the northern roof area bent in slightly, the vertex and the southern roofage arched up and bulged out at the same time. then i pulled the momentum of the northern roof over the ridge, down a bit to the south and decoupled the roof areas with a row of skylights that shadow themselves on account of the inclination.' the further conclusion drawn in the homeopathically dynamized rigid system was to open the faces with wedge-formed glass panes running from the roof to the ground. the skeleton consists of three-hinged frames of curved glulam beams set on steel columns that are perforated at load-diverting spots for the tubes of a hot-air heating system. the envelope consists of insulated steel panels and trapezoidal sheet metal lining.

from standstill to one hundred in 8 cm
von null auf hundert in 8 cm

ausgangspunkt war ein baureifes investorenprojekt in gestalt einer ländlichen scheune. für wolfgang krejs, den lokalen baudirektor, war das ambitionslose volumen an einer haupteinfahrt der stadt nicht akzeptabel, er forderte eine änderung unter einbeziehung eines architekten. für sam war der spielraum ökonomisch und räumlich minimal: ‚ich konnte vom querschnitt mit dem satteldach kaum 8 cm abweichen. meine intervention war sehr einfach: ich drückte zunächst gleichsam von oben auf die nordseitige dachfläche. dadurch verformte sich die ganze struktur. die nördliche dachfläche bog sich leicht nach innen, der scheitel und mit ihm die südliche dachfläche wölbte sich simultan nach oben und außen. dann zog ich den schwung der nördlichen dachfläche über den first hinaus, etwas nach süden hinunter und entkoppelte die dachflächen mit einem oberlichtband, das durch die neigung sich selbst beschattet.‘ die weitere konsequenz der homöopathischen dynamisierung des starren systems war das öffnen der stirnseiten mit keilförmigen, vom dach bis zum boden verlaufenden glasflächen. das tragskelett bilden dreigelenksrahmen aus geschweiften leimbindern auf stahlstützen, die im bereich der lastumleitung für die rohre der luftheizung perforiert sind. die hülle besteht aus gedämmten stahlkassetten und trapezblechverkleidung.

concept draft; east side; interior
konzeptskizze; ostseite; innenraum

mitterau indoor tennis court
tennishalle mitterau

detail façade; support glulam beams
detail fassade; auflager der leimbinder

view from the north, gangway to clubhouse
übersicht von norden, gangway zum klubhaus

dr. resch dwelling, conversion of a medieval manor, krems/rehberg, 1ˢᵗ phase of construction 2001
wohnhaus dr. resch, umbau eines mittelalterlichen gutshofs, 1. bauabschnitt

the medieval farm of stone face masonry with a free-standing black kitchen and a pyramidal chimney is unique in the region and classified as a historical monument. the new owner saw the hendrik bar and commissioned sam to adapt the manor for his family. this 'work in progress' follows the maxim to do the least possible damage to the original substance. the hermetic volume's openings are set in an extremely lapidary fashion and improved in efficiency by interior light deflections. a new supporting structure as high as the old spatial quadrant was engrafted in the l-wing's bend. two delicate, silhouetted concrete slabs interweave with two other slabs, like two pairs of arms forming a mountaineer's tragsitz, such that they join in on the thousand-year-old outer walls of stone at four points only. this structure supports the elevator, stairways, new walls and floors; the old ceiling joists were preserved and 'penetrate' the correspondingly perforated concrete walls. all new implants, interior and exterior, are detached from the old building, are materially and constructively concentrated and elementary, bringing about a state of tension between the old and the new, an energy field of contrasts that relate most closely to one another in spite of the distance. the age-old material is thus amazingly accelerated into the present and today's conciseness densified into 'timeless' incisiveness.

relativity of time
relativität von zeit

der mittelalterliche bauernhof aus steinsichtmauern mit freistehender rauchküche und pyramidenkamin ist für die region ein unikat, denkmalgeschützt. der neue besitzer sah die bar hendrik und beauftragte sam mit der adaptierung des hofes für seine familie. das ,work in progress‘ folgt der maxime, die originäre substanz nur minimal zu verletzen. öffnungen in das hermetische volumen werden extrem lapidar gesetzt und durch lichtumlenkungen im inneren effizienter gemacht. in der beuge des l-traktes wird dem alten raumquadranten in voller höhe eine neue tragstruktur eingepflanzt. zwei papierdünne, scherenschnitthafte betonscheiben sind mit zwei weiteren scheiben wie der bekannte tragsitz aus armpaaren so miteinander verflochten, dass sie in die tausendjährigen außenwände aus stein nur an vier punkten eingreifen. diese struktur trägt lift, treppe, neue wände und böden; die alten deckenbalken blieben erhalten und ,durchstoßen‘ die entsprechend perforierten betonwände. alle neuen implantate, innen wie außen, sind vom altbau gelöst, sind materiell und konstruktiv so konzentriert und elementar, dass zwischen alt und neu eine spannung entsteht, ein energiefeld der trotz distanz engstens aufeinander bezogenen kontraste. so wird die uralte materie verblüffend in die gegenwart beschleunigt und das heutige in eine ,zeitlose‘ prägnanz verdichtet.

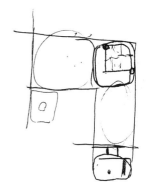

draft balcony annex; detail stairway; situation
skizze balkonzubau; detail stiege; situation

kunstmeile krems façade, in collaboration with irene ott-reinisch, lower austria, 2001
fassade kunstmeile krems, in zusammenarbeit mit irene ott-reinisch

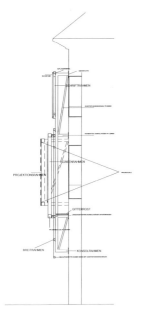

variable info layer along the newly occupied industrial body
variable info-schicht am neu genutzten industriebau

franz sam
franz-josefs-kai 45/6, a–1010 wien
tel +43-532 81 84-15, fax +43-532 81 84-11
architekt.sam.kai@aon.at

franz sam, born in 1956 in tiefenfucha, lower austria; studied architecture at innsbruck tu, awarded diploma in 1984. assistance and research at the department of building construction at innsbruck tu, 1981–85. project leader with coop himmelb(l)au, 1985–92. architects office since 1992. assistant, university of applied arts, wolf d. prix master class, vienna, since 1994. vice president of the chamber of architecture for vienna, lower austria and burgenland since 1998.

buildings, projects (select): hendrik bar, 1993–95; mitterau indoor tennis court, 1996–97, both in krems, lower austria; stelzer office building, herzogenburg, lower austria, 1996–2001; design for emmersdorf square (competition in 2000, 1st prize), 2000–01; sacha/katzensteiner law office, krems, 2001. under construction: dr. resch dwelling, conversion of a medieval manor; reither house, attic development; all in krems, lower austria. planned: göls dwelling, krems, lower austria; vinotheque, bregenz, vorarlberg; funeral parlor, großmugl, lower austria.

franz sam, geboren 1956 in tiefenfucha, nö; architekturstudium an der tu innsbruck, diplom 1984; 1981–85 studienassistenz und forschungsarbeit am institut für hochbau an der tu innsbruck. 1985–92 projektleitung bei coop himmelb(l)au. seit 1992 eigenes architekturbüro. seit 1994 hochschulassistent, hochschule für angewandte kunst, meisterklasse prix, wien. seit 1998 vizepräsident der architektenkammer für wien, niederösterreich und burgenland.

bauten, projekte (auswahl): 1993–95 bar hendrik; 1996–97 tennishalle mitterau; beide krems, nö. 1996–2001 bürogebäude stelzer, herzogenburg, nö; 2000–01 platzgestaltung emmersdorf (wettbewerb, 1. preis, 2000); 2001 anwaltskanzlei sacha/katzensteiner, krems. in bau: wohnhaus dr. resch, umbau eines mittelalterlichen gutshofs; haus reither, dachgeschoßausbau, beide in krems. in planung: wohnhaus göls, krems; vinothek bregenz, vorarlberg; aufbahrungshalle, großmugl, nö.

stelzer office building / bürogebäude stelzer, herzogenburg

client / bauherr: di hans stelzer

collaborators / mitarbeiterinnen: karin sam, elfriede hopfner

statics / statik: retter & partner

building contractor/ bauunternehmen: fa. stelzer

structural steelwork / stahlbau: fa. jordanits

interior / einrichtung: bene büromöbel

sacha/katzensteiner law office / anwaltskanzlei sacha/katzensteiner, krems

client / bauherr: dr. hubert sacha, mag. günther katzensteiner

collaborator / mitarbeiter: stefan filler

building contractor/ bauunternehmen: fa. bischof

dry construction / trockenbau: fa. surböck

glasswork / verglasungen: fa. schober

interior / einrichtung: bene büromöbel

hendrik bar / bar hendrik, krems

client / bauherr: arend and / und gerrit timmerman

collaborators / mitarbeiter: karin sam, robert stojek

joiner / tischler: fa. rehor

locksmith / schlosser: fa. danner

mitterau indoor tennis court / tennishalle mitterau, krems

client / bauherr: tenniscenter krems mitterau gesmbh / manfred rohrböck

collaborators / mitarbeiterinnen: karin sam, elfriede hopfner

statics / statik: karl heinz hollinsky

building contractor / bauunternehmen: fa. schubrig

construction / konstruktion: fa. glöckel, fa. nestler

dr. resch dwelling, conversion of a medieval manor, 1st phase of construction / wohnhaus

dr. resch, umbau eines mittelalterlichen gutshofs, 1. bauabschnitt, krems/rehberg

client / bauherr: dr. reinhard and / und dr. erika resch

collaborators / mitarbeiter: stefan filler, helga heinl, irene ott-reinisch

building inspection / bauaufsicht: harald schlager

building contractor / bauunternehmen: fa. schroll

structural steelwork / stahlbau: fa. jordanits

engineering of services / haustechnik: fa. bayer, fa. berger

kunstmeile krems façade, in collaboration with irene ott-reinisch / fassade kunstmeile krems,

in zusammenarbeit mit irene ott-reinisch

client / bauherr: amt der nö landesregierung / abteilung für kunst und wissenschaft

structural steelwork / stahlbau: fa. jordanits

screens: fa. plakativ

with the kind support of / mit freundlicher unterstützung von:

josef glöckel gesmbh, siedlungsstraße 12, a–3200 obergrafendorf

sacha + katzensteiner rechtsanwälte oeg dr, gartenaugasse 3, a–3500 krems a. d. donau

architekturzentrum wien; springer-verlag wien new york; text: © otto kapfinger

photo credits: © by the architect and: irene ott-reinisch: 225; alexander rajchl: 217–219, 221–223, 225;

margherita spiluttini: 205, 207, 209, 211–215, 226

weichlbauer/ortis

in general, the architecture scene has banally acknowledged postmodernity as a cultural condition. weichlbauer / ortis are among the few planners in austria who attempt to practice the postmodern principle of ambivalence as a form of living and an operational method at today's intellectual level. they are up to (virtually) all the tricks of chaos theory, fuzzy logic, the theories of data processing, science and architecture. however, they consciously beware of obvious extremes: the extreme to turn such instruments against its inherent logic by applying them in terms of conventional modernity in order to create 'innovative' forms or new 'styles'; or the other extreme that would see subjective decision-making or intuition fully eliminated from form-finding processes. weichlbauer / ortis lead double-encoded lives in which one directs a contracting company while the other teaches at a building school, to join forces in a parallel existence and be able to 'afford' outings into conceptional architecture. according to their understanding, the knowledge of 'fractally determined space' is no real urge to seek inventions of 'fractal' forms, but rather a qualification for new, open insights into and arrangements of influence factors and levels of reality. on the other hand, they employ computer programs and random generators at the beginning and in between planning steps. their objective is to fade out subjective preferences and internalized schematisms at the very root

ambivalence advances
ambivalenz avanciert

postmodernität als kultureller zustand wurde in der architekturszene meist banal rezipiert. weichlbauer / ortis zählen in österreich zu den wenigen planern, die das postmoderne prinzip der ambivalenz als lebensform und arbeitsmethode auf dem intellektuellen niveau der zeit zu praktizieren versuchen. sie sind wohl mit (fast) allen wassern der chaostheorie, der fuzzy logic, der computer-, wissenschafts- und architekturtheorien gewaschen. sie hüten sich aber bewusst vor den naheliegenden extremen: vor jenem extrem, das solche instrumentarien gegen deren inhärente logik kehrt, indem sie diese im sinne konventioneller modernität zur kreation ‚innovativer' formen oder neuer ‚stile' beansprucht; und vor dem anderen, das die subjektive entscheidung oder intuition gleich gänzlich aus dem formfindungsprozess eliminiert sehen will. weichlbauer / ortis leben die doppelkodierte existenz, der eine als leiter einer baufirma, der andere als lehrer an einer baufachschule, um sich als team in parallelexistenz periodische ausflüge in die konzeptionelle architektur zu ‚leisten'. das wissen um den ‚fraktal bestimmten raum' drängt in ihrem verständnis nicht zur suche nach ‚fraktalen' formerfindungen, sondern befähigt zu einem neuen, offeneren sehen und ordnen von einflussfaktoren und realitätsebenen. umgekehrt benutzen sie computerprogramme und zufallsgeneratoren am beginn und in zwischenphasen von planungsschritten, um sozusagen

repacking, residential building, st. lorenzen, 1998
neuverpackung, wohnbau

of design decisions, to let their own interpretation intervene in the mechanically triggered process, carrying on in a declared and selectively intuitive fashion. with different intensities – varying from the art gallery project to low-cost estates – they overlay computer-generated para-meters, site plans and arrangements of volumes with the purely applied standards of building reality, with industrial ready-mades from other contexts. construction units are homogenized to the least possible com-ponents, individual elements used without change for various 'functions', etc. – measures that altogether counteract the clear-cut syntax of functionalistic or formalistic differentiation. an estate may consist of houses, as though taken from children's drawings, topped by a steep roof type given an industrially fabricated 'carrosserie' of corrugated sheets and conditioned interiorly for the benefit of a rich polyvalence; a bidet by colani may serve as a washbowl, the hue shown by a standard switch may cover a house's entire interior structure, and so on. weichlbauer/ortis cherish neither nostalgic nor futuristic romance, refrain from arguing in terms of 'right or wrong'. they use advanced methods and diagrams of science in an attempt to open novel, irritating visual corridors into the routine of the construction industry.

an der basis von entwurfsentscheidungen subjektive vorlieben und internalisierte schematismen auszublenden, um dann in den maschinell angelaufenen prozess mit ihrer interpretation deklariert weiterführend und selektiv-intuitiv einzugreifen. in unterschiedlicher intensität, vom kunsthausprojekt bis zur lowcost-siedlung überlagern sie computer-generierte parameter, lagepläne, volumensdispositionen mit pur einge-setzten standards der baurealität, mit industriellen readymades aus anderen kontexten. die bauglieder werden auf möglichst wenige ein-zelteile homogenisiert, einzelne elemente unverändert für verschiedene ‚funktionen' verwendet etc. – alles maßnahmen, um der eindeutigen syntax funktionalistischer oder formalistischer differenzierung entgegen-zuwirken. eine siedlung kann aus häusern wie von kinderhand ge-zeichnet bestehen, wobei der steildachtyp aber eine industriell gefertigte ‚karosserie' aus wellplatten erhält und innenräumlich für eine reiche polyvalenz konditioniert ist; ein colani-bidet kann als handwaschbecken dienen, der farbton eines normschalters kann die gesamte innenstruktur eines hauses überziehen usw.. weichlbauer/ortis frönen weder der nostalgischen noch der futuristischen romantik, argumentieren nicht ‚richtig oder falsch'. sie benutzen avancierte methoden und wissen-schaftsdiagramme, um neue, irritierende blickkorridore in den bauindu-striellen alltag zu eröffnen.

art block, iron house, competition project, graz, 2000
kunstblock, eisernes haus, wettbewerbsprojekt

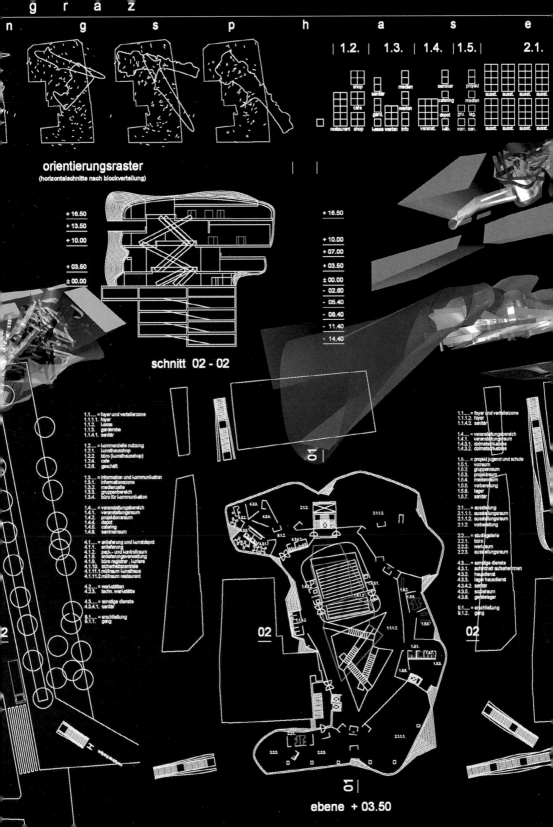

g r a z ... n g s p h a s e

| 1.2. | 1.3. | 1.4. | 1.5. | 2.1.

orientierungsraster
(horizontalschnitte nach blockverteilung)

schnitt 02 - 02

ebene + 03.50

movable plastering
beweglicher verputz

the building is located on the city's outskirts; single-family and multi-family dwellings with high steep roofs, rural constructions, in the neighborhood; the decorated box accommodating a local shopping mall right across, a much frequented street that suffers from a daytime noise level of 63 db and 54 db at night in between. the private building sponsor defined the occupancy with apartments to be rented to nomadic laptop workers or working students for determinable periods of time, intermixed with office areas, and drew up a minimal cost estimate. a monolithic block is the answer to the stressed location and fluctuating program – flat, dark blue and hermetic, set at a maximal distance to the street. an optically and effectively protected refuge for short-term dwelling and working, smoothly closeable on the street side with noise-insulating sliding shutters. a highly flexible hall-type building in structural terms, showing few interior benchmarks, placed between a hotel and loft, and equipped in a lapidary fashion. the architects see the row separated from the street by traffic, parking and green lanes as a 'rush hour'/'blue hour' hybrid, somewhere between spatial consolidation and optical evaporation. the only intricate, yet important detail in this concept: the sliding shutters are also coated with the facing plaster to support the skin's homogeneity.

der bau steht am stadtrand; in der nachbarschaft ein- und mehrfamilienhäuser mit hohen steildächern, rurale bauten; gegenüber die dekorierte schachtel des lokalen einkaufszentrums, dazwischen eine hochfrequentierte straße mit 63 db lärmpegel am tag und 54 db in der nacht. der private bauträger definierte die nutzung mit befristet vermietbaren wohnungen für nomadische laptop-arbeiter oder werkstudenten, durchmischt mit büroflächen, und erstellte einen minimalen kostenrahmen. die antwort auf den stressbelasteten ort und das fluktuierende programm ist ein monolithischer block – flach, dunkelblau und hermetisch, mit maximaler distanz zur straße gelagert. ein optisch und faktisch geschützter zufluchtsort zum kurzfristigen bewohnen und arbeiten, zur straße mit schallschutz-schiebeläden nahtlos verschließbar, strukturell ein hallenbau von hoher flexibilität mit wenigen inneren fixpunkten, angesiedelt zwischen hotel und loft, in der ausstattung lapidar. die architekten sehen die mit fahr-, park- und grünstreifen von der straße abgesetzte zeile als hybrid zwischen ‚rush hour' und ‚blue hour', zwischen räumlicher verfestigung und optischer verflüchtigung. einziges kniffliges, doch in diesem konzept wichtiges detail: für die homogenität der außenhaut sind auch die schiebeläden mit dem fassadenputz überzogen.

zoning of area in front; volume in context
zonierung vorbereich; volumen im kontext

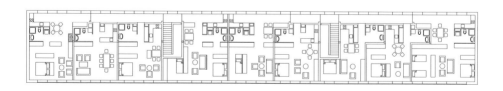

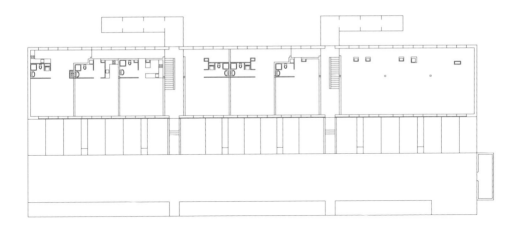

upper floor; staircase; façade detail street side; ground floor
obergeschoß; stiegendetail; fassadendetail straßenseite; erdgeschoß

family shelves, frohnleiten, styria, 1995–99
familienregal

dialectical residential
dialektisches wohnregal

the house stands crossways in a long-drawn plot, it separates and links two large garden areas. the two-story concrete stirrup marks the location, frames the space. exterior space penetrates deeply into the framed volume along the open and fully paned long sides. there are no walls within the glazings, shaded by the concrete lining, but only floor-to-floor cabinet elements that are graded in parallel. set off from the glazing by the loggias' width, they accommodate the entire infrastructure and can be closed as 'rooms within a room', if necessary, by accordion doors. like a loft, the interior thus offers a diversely passable and usable continuum with an optical range that extends to the walls marking off the gardens. solar-controlled awnings on the outside of the loggias and curtains on the inside of the glass faces serve as temporary visual and light filters. reminiscent of shelves, of furniture, the indoor deco-ration is given the electrical switch's glimmering, broken white shade, moving the awnings and curtains, guiding the light, energy and climate. in terms of dimensional rhythms, as well, this dematerialized inner life is detached from the presence of supporting concrete frame and glass separators. nikolaus hellmayr was to refer to 'dialectical family shelves' that address classical themes – and repeatedly work against the grain.

das haus steht quer im langgestreckten grund, es trennt und verknüpft zwei große gartenbereiche. der zweigeschoßige betonbügel markiert den ort, rahmt den raum. an den ganz in glas geöffneten längsseiten dringt der außenraum tief in das gerahmte volumen ein. innerhalb der vom betonmantel beschatteten verglasungen gibt es keine wände, sondern nur parallel gestaffelte, raumhohe schrankelemente. sie sind von den gläsern um die loggienbreite nach innen abgesetzt, enthalten die gesamte infrastruktur und können mit falttüren je nach bedarf zu ,räumen im raum' verschlossen werden. so bietet der innenraum wie ein loft ein vielfältig begehbares und nutzbares kontinuum, dessen optische reichweite aber bis an die grenzwände des gartens geht. als temporäre blick- und lichtfilter dienen solargesteuerte markisen an der außenseite der loggien und vorhänge an der innenseite der glasfronten. die ganze regal- und möbelhafte innenausstattung hat den schim-mernden, gebrochenen weißton der elektrischen schalter, welche die markisen und vorhänge bewegen, licht, energie und klima regeln. auch in den maßlichen rhythmen ist diese entstofflichte innenwelt von der präsenz des tragenden betonrahmens und den glasteilungen gelöst. nikolaus hellmayr nannte es ein ,dialektisches familienregal', das klassische themen anspricht – und mehrfach gegen den strich bürstet.

open concrete frame, stacked inside-outside crossing
offener betonrahmen, geschichteter übergang außen/innen

family shelves
familienregal

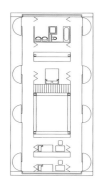

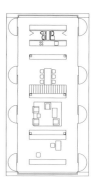

concept diagrams; ground plans, frame open on both sides, shelves inserted
konzeptdiagramme; grundrisse, beidseitig offener rahmen, eingestellte regale

ambivalence

appearances alone are undeceived

nur der schein trügt nicht

austria's craziest rental housing of the nineties. a clear semidetached dwelling with open ground plans and large individual free spaces, at once a sardonic elaboration of basic conditions. the construction is located between smooth tier buildings to the northwest and structurally divided, low single-family dwellings to the southeast. following the initially approved scheme, replanning became necessary after a change in the kind of support in adherence to the other premises. playing according to the new rules, the architects continued a design game that had been initiated in the primary phase with computer-generated patterns. the result is multiply ambivalent. it is everyday and cheerful, peculiar and unfathomable all at the same time. the building indeed has quite real functions – but then, aspects virtually capsize into unreality. it is homogeneous and isotropic on the inside, hybrid and dislocated on the outside: an obviously three-story smooth block to the north, a low, extreme plasticity to the south, balconies pulled out like drawers, a homogeneous, violent bright yellow skin that arrests the optics of a powerful motion. at second glance, there is only one window format, one door format and one balcony element, also serving as a marquee, a roof for the parking spaces and balcony, a terrace giving to the front yard. all's alike but not the same. a chameleon born of the most simple components. all's functional, but nothing what it seems to be.

in österreich der verrückteste mietwohnbau der neunziger jahre. ein klarer zweispänner mit offenen grundrissen und großen individuellen freiplätzen, zugleich eine sardonische durcharbeitung von randbedingungen. der bau steht zwischen glatten geschoßbauten im nordwesten und gegliederten, niedrigen einfamilienhäusern im südosten. nach der ersten, genehmigten planung musste durch einen wechsel der förderungsart unter einhaltung der übrigen prämissen umgeplant werden. unter den neuen spielregeln setzten die architekten ein in der primärphase mit computergenerierten mustern begonnenes entwurfsspiel fort. das resultat ist mehrfach ambivalent. es ist alltäglich und heiter und zugleich skurril und abgründig. der bau funktioniert ganz real, zugleich kippen aspekte gleichsam ins irreale. er ist innen homogen und isotrop, außen hybrid und disloziert: nordseitig ein offenbar dreigeschoßiger, glatter block, südseitig eine niedrigere, extreme plastizität, wie schubladen herausgezogene balkone, doch die starke bewegung durch die homogene, knallgelbe haut optisch angehalten. beim nächsten blick stellt sich heraus: es gibt nur ein fensterformat, ein türformat und ein balkonelement, und dieses fungiert auch als eingangsvordach, als stellplatzdach, als balkondach und auch als terrasse am vorgarten. alles ist gleich und nichts dasselbe. ein chamäleon aus simpelsten teilen. alles funktioniert, aber nichts ist, was es scheint.

computer-generated development of the body

computergenerierte entwicklung des baukörpers

advances

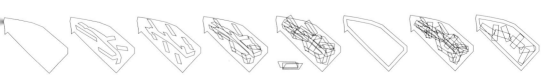

roofed parking spaces along the house
gedeckte stellplätze am haus

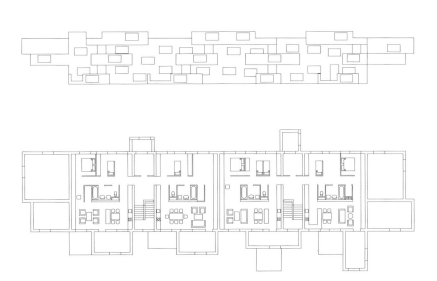

ground plan upper story, façade; southern view
grundriss obergeschoß, fassade; südansicht

how the form is born
wie die form entsteht

weichlbauer/ortis have set forth new design processes in numerous projects for dwelling quarters and larger urban tasks. they work with computer-generated 'random events' in an attempt to exceed typical planning methods. at the beginning of a project, for instance, computer-made patterns are scattered into the site plans, superposed with values and varied mathematically. the resulting abstract and extremely vivid form figures are intended to assist in intensifying empathy for the location and breaking open the normativeness of traditional typologies. in subsequent phases, the usual parameters – sun and shade diagrams, alignments – are fed into this fractal game, yet the structure's concrete form is left as undetermined as possible to the end. in addition to the plot itself, the base material used for the kunsthaus graz included the results of past competitions (trigon museum, museum im berg), the geometries of which were 'plowed' into the new project's basis and processed further. following the montessori method in the case of the system kindergarten, polyvalent spatial modules for the most diverse properties are combined in an arithmetically optimal way and covered with the roof pitches' geometries that develop especially from combinatorics.

in etlichen projekten für wohnquartiere und größere urbane aufgaben haben weichlbauer/ortis neue entwurfsvorgänge dargestellt. sie arbeiten mit computergenerierten, ‚zufälligen ereignissen‘, um über die gewohnten planungsmethoden hinauszugehen. so werden am beginn eines projekts in den lageplänen vom computer erzeugte muster verteilt, diese mit kennwerten überlagert und rechnerisch variiert. die so entstehenden abstrakten und zugleich äußerst lebendigen formgebilde sollen helfen, das einfühlungsvermögen für den ort zu schärfen und die normativität tradierter typologien aufzubrechen. in weiteren phasen werden in dieses fraktale spiel die üblichen parameter – sonnen- und schattendiagramme, fluchtlinien etc. – eingespeist, die konkretisierung der baugestalt wird aber bis zuletzt möglichst offen gehalten. beim kunsthaus graz dienten als ausgangsmaterial zusätzlich zum grundstück die ergebnisse der vorher abgelaufenen wettbewerbe (trigon museum, museum im berg), deren geometrien in die basis des neuen projekts ‚eingeackert‘ und weiterverarbeitet wurden. beim systemkindergarten werden analog zur montessoripädagogik polyvalente raummodule für verschiedenste grundstücke rechnerisch optimal kombiniert und mit den aus dieser kombinatorik jeweils speziell entstandenen geometrien von dachflächen überdeckt.

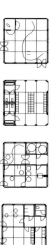

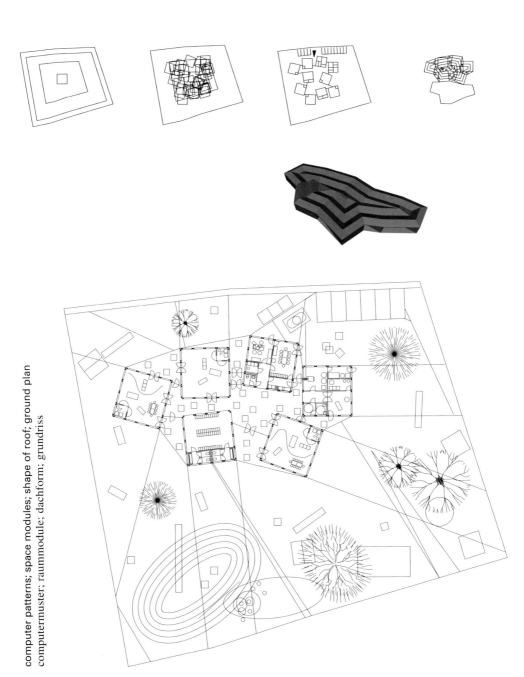

computer patterns; space modules; shape of roof; ground plan
computermuster; raummodule; dachform; grundriss

a reanimated carcass ruin from the seventies. the building was conceived for a hatter but never completed. the situation is rural-alpine and
occupied by traditional detached houses, the property directly borders
on a protected zone codified by formal building regulations. already
dilapidated, the carcass was reorganized inside for living units and
'repacked' on the outside with a spatial and thermal envelope. the
volume's trite typology including a saddle roof and balcony galleries was
thus radicalized from a motive character to structural consistency. the
balconies' cantilever plates were supplemented with a wooden construction to form a continuous spatial layer serving access and private
free spaces. the plates were wrapped in a translucent waterproofing,
together with the newly insulated roof that was given new openings.
the homogeneous jacket of pvc panels is equipped with openable
sections to provide optimal lighting and ventilation. this inexpensive,
robust material is commonly used in the country to cover annexes, stock
rooms, silos and gardens. the ambivalent veil actualizes and modifies
the old morphology, discloses the industrial reality of today's 'rurality',
as a dwelling's façade that even excels the allegorical form of old barn
constructions in its homogeneous appearance.

repacking as an oxymoron
verpackung als oxymoron

wiederbelebung einer rohbauruine aus den siebziger jahren. der bau
war als betriebsstätte für eine huterzeugung konzipiert, wurde aber nie
fertiggestellt. die situation ist dörflich-alpin mit traditionellen einzel-
häusern, der grund grenzt direkt an eine durch formale bauregeln
kodierte schutzzone. der bereits schadhafte rohbau wurde innen für
wohneinheiten neu organisiert und außen mit einer räumlichen und
thermischen hülle ‚neu verpackt'. die klischeehafte typologie des
volumens mit satteldach und balkongalerien wurde damit vom motivi-
schen zu einer strukturellen konsequenz radikalisiert. die vorhandenen
kragplatten für balkone wurden mit einer holzkonstruktion zur kon-
tinuierlichen raumschicht für erschließung und private freibereiche
ergänzt und diese wie auch das neu gedämmte und mit neuen öffnungen
versehene dach mit einem transluzenten wetterschutz umhüllt. das
homogene kleid aus pvc-platten ist mit öffenbaren partien für optimale
belichtung und durchlüftung versehen. dieses billige, robuste material
wird am land gewöhnlich für die abdeckung von anbauten, von lagern,
silos oder gartenanlagen verwendet. als fassade eines wohngebäudes,
das in seiner homogenen erscheinung die zeichenhaftigkeit alter
stadelbauten noch übertrifft, aktualisiert und relativiert der ambivalente
schleier die alte morphologie, enthüllt er die industrielle wirklichkeit
heutiger ‚ländlichkeit'.

view in the rural context
ansicht im ländlichen kontext

advances

repacking, residential building
neuverpackung, wohnbau

between cover and core
zwischen hülle und kern

weichlbauer / ortis
mauritzener hauptstraße 3, a–8130 frohnleiten
tel +43-3126-4510, fax +43-3126-4510
reinholdweichlbauer@aon.at, ortis@utanet.at

reinhold weichlbauer, born in bruck/mur, styria, in 1962; secondary
school of technology (htbla) 1977–82, graz tu, awarded diploma in 1989
and civil engineer's license in 1994; teaching assignment at graz htbla
since 1998.
albert josef ortis, born in graz in 1961; htbla 1976–81, graz tu, awarded
diploma in 1990 and civil engineer's license in 1994; assistant at graz tu
1990–96.
buildings, projects (select): 1991–2001: austria 1000 terminal, vienna;
residential fracture, neudörfl, burgenland; residential tool, frohnleiten;
residential settlement, st. bartholomä; consulting office anatomy,
st. oswald; family shelves, frohnleiten; repacking, residential building,
st. lorenzen; residential transformation, deutschlandsberg; residential
DNA, gratkorn; system kindergarten, peggau; school diagram, stainach;
all in styria. urban heartbeat; tool modulation; villa game; residential
irritation; w#plus; art block, iron house; office implant; all in graz.
architecture reparation, liverpool, great britain; dwelling mobility,
giubiasco, switzerland; energy game house, tokyo; hybrid structure,
tallinn, estonia.

reinhold weichlbauer, geboren 1962 in bruck/mur; htbla 1977–82,
tu graz, diplom 1989, ziviltechnikerbefugnis 1994, lehrverpflichtung
htbla graz seit 1998.
albert josef ortis, geboren 1961 in graz; htbla 1976–81, tu graz,
diplom 1990, ziviltechnikerbefugnis 1994, assistent an der tu graz
1990–96.
bauten, projekte (auswahl): 1991–2001: austria 1000 terminal, wien;
wohnfraktal, neudörfl, burgenland. wohngerät, frohnleiten; wohn-
siedlung, st. bartholomä; ordinationsanatomie, st. oswald; familienregal,
frohnleiten; neuverpackung, wohnbau, st. lorenzen; wohntrans-
formation, deutschlandsberg; wohnDNA, gratkorn; systemkindergarten,
peggau; schuldiagramm, stainach; alle steiermark. städtischer herz-
schlag; werkzeugmodulation; villenspiel; wohnirritation; w#plus;
kunstblock, eisernes haus; büroimplantat; alle graz. architektur-
reparatur, liverpool, großbritannien; behausungsmobilität, giubiasco,
schweiz; energy game house, tokio; hybridstruktur, tallinn, estland.

proj.nr. 199602 repacking, residential building / neuverpackung, wohnbau, st. lorenzen

client / bauherr: ortis immobilien & bauträgergesmbh, frohnleiten

statics / statik: di gerhard fidler, graz

engineering of services / haustechnik: büro hammer, judenburg

proj.nr 200001 art block, iron house, competition / kunstblock, eisernes haus, graz, wettbewerb

client / bauherr: city of graz / stadt graz

proj.nr. 199605 residential irritation / wohnirritation, graz

client / bauherr: di christian soos, graz

statics / statik: di gerhard fidler, graz

engineering of services / haustechnik: büro maxones, graz

proj.nr. 199503 family shelves / familienregal, frohnleiten

client / bauherr: familie ortis, frohnleiten

statics / statik: di dr. techn. kurt kratzer, graz

engineering of services / haustechnik: büro hammer, judenburg

consultant / konsulent: elektro rössler, voitsberg

garden / garten: di dr. wilhelm prem, graz

proj.nr. 199806 residential DNA / wohnDNA, gratkorn

client / bauherr: leykam gemeinnützige wohn-, bau- und siedlungsgesmbh, gratkorn

statics / statik: di madjid fazeli, di johann wolfesberger, graz

construction physics / bauphysik: ing. johann brodacz, graz

engineering of services / haustechnik: büro hammer, judenburg

proj.nr. 199901 system kindergarten, competition / systemkindergarten, peggau, wettbewerb

client / bauherr: styrian building guild / landesinnung der baugewerbe steiermark, graz

architekturzentrum wien; springer-verlag wien new york; text: © otto kapfinger

photo credits: © by the architects and: peter eder: 229, 231, 235–237, 239–241, 243–245, 249, 250

Exhibition Venues to Date
Ausstellungsstationen

Emerging Architecture 1
Kommende Architektur 1
10 Austrian Offices

21. 09. 2000 – 30. 10. 2000
Architekturzentrum Wien, Vienna / Wien

18. 01. 2001 – 18. 03. 2001
Danish Centre for Architecture – Gammel Dok, Copenhagen / Kopenhagen

19. 05. 2001 – 05. 08. 2001
Deutsches Architektur Museum – DAM, Frankfurt/Main

14. 09. 2001 – 14. 10. 2001
Fonó Budai Zenehaz, Budapest

16. 01. 2002 – 06. 02. 2002
Austrian Cultural Forum Rome / Österreichisches Kulturforum Rom:
'mittelarchitetture. Dialoghi d'architettura fra Austria e Italia'
(curator/Kurator: Alberto Alessi): A series of dialogs accompanied by a
video and book presentation / Eine Gesprächsreihe mit Video- und
Buchpräsentation

Emerging Architecture 2
Kommende Architektur 2
10 More Austrians

06. 12. 2001 – 15. 04. 2002
Architekturzentrum Wien, Vienna / Wien

13. 10. 2002 – 20. 10. 2002
MEO-Contemporary Art Collection, Budapest

Emerging Architecture 3
Kommende Architektur 3
Beyond Architainment

21. 11. 2002 – 10. 03. 2003
Architekturzentrum Wien, Vienna / Wien

Gabriele Kaiser, born in 1967, freelance architectural journalist for 'Architektur aktuell', 'Baumeister', 'l'architécture d'aujourd'hui', 'oris', et al. Lecturer at the University of Applied Arts in Vienna. Editorial activities for the Architektur Archiv Austria, the online database of the Architekturzentrum Wien (together with Kurt Zweifel).

Otto Kapfinger, born in 1949, freelance architectural journalist; co-founder of 'Missing Link' in 1970, editor of 'UMBAU' from 1979–90; architectural critic in 'Die Presse' from 1981–90; authored 25 books and catalogs on 20ᵗʰ-century architecture in Austria, curator of 15 specialist exhibitions; member of the design commissions in the cities of Salzburg and Krems from 1997–2000.

With the kind support of / Mit freundlicher Unterstützung von
Bundeskanzleramt Sektion Kunst; Bundesministerium für Bildung, Wissenschaft und Kultur;
Geschäftsgruppe Stadtentwicklung und Verkehr; UNIQA Versicherungen AG; Wien Kultur;
Zumtobel Staff Österreich Vertriebs-GmbH

This book is published on the occasion of the exhibition Emerging Architecture 3 arranged by /
Diese Publikation erscheint zur Ausstellung Kommende Architektur 3, veranstaltet vom
Architekturzentrum Wien, 21. 11. 2002 – 10. 3. 2003

General concept and text / Gesamtkonzept, Auswahl und Texte: Otto Kapfinger
Project management and editorial work / Projektkoordination und Redaktion: Susanne Jäger

Exhibition / Ausstellung:
Design exhibition sets: art specials*, Kurt Olli Aigner, Wolfgang Stückler
Panel design: Gabriele Lenz
Videos: ZONE, Wien

Publication / Katalogbuch:
Edited by / Herausgegeben von: Architekturzentrum Wien
Series concept and graphic design / Reihenkonzept und Gestaltung: Gabriele Lenz
Collaborator / Mitarbeit: Ewa Kaja
Support: Elmar Bertsch
Translation / Übersetzung: Karl Thomanek
Consultant / Konsulent: Mark Gilbert
Copy-editing / Lektorat: Claudia Mazanek
Printer / Druck: A. Holzhausens Nfg., A–1140 Wien
Printed on acid-free and chlorine-free bleached paper / Gedruckt auf säurefreiem, chlorfrei
gebleichtem Papier-TCF
SPIN: 10867917

© 2003 Architekturzentrum Wien, Springer-Verlag/Wien
Printed in Austria

Bibliografische Information Der Deutschen Bibliothek
Die Deutsche Bibliothek verzeichnet diese Publikation in der Deutschen Nationalbibliografie;
detaillierte bibliografische Daten sind im Internet über <http://dnb.ddb.de> abrufbar.

Note: text spelt with small letters complies with the architects' request. / Auf Wunsch einiger
Architekten(teams) sind die betreffenden Texte in Kleinschreibung gehalten.